CHRISTIAN TRUTH

CHRISTIAN TRUTH

JOHN COVENTRY, S.J.

Lecturer in Christian Doctrine,
Heythrop College (University of London)

Paulist Press
New York, N.Y./Paramus, N.J.

First published in Great Britain in 1975 by
Darton, Longman & Todd Ltd
85 Gloucester Road, London SW7 4SU

© John Coventry, 1975

De licentia Superiorum Ordinis

Copyright © 1975 by
The Missionary Society
of St. Paul the Apostle
in the State of New York

ISBN: 0-8091-1903-X

COVER DESIGN: Morris Berman

Published by Paulist Press
Editorial Office: 1865 Broadway, N.Y., N.Y. 10023
Business Office: 400 Sette Drive, Paramus, N.J. 07652

Printed and bound in the
United States of America

CONTENTS

6. TEACHING OFFICE IN THE CHURCH

7. THE BIBLE IN THE CHURCH

Chapter One

FAITH IN CHRIST

(a) *The faith of the apostolic eye-witnesses*

Older attempts within catholic theology to show how christian faith works, and thereby to make clear its ground or basis,
operated with what is now called a propositional view of
faith – the assumption that faith is primarily or basically a
matter of assent to doctrines – and got themselves into something of a tangle in the process.[1] It can now safely be assumed
within the same catholic tradition that the key to understanding faith is the realisation that faith is basically in Christ, and
that any assent to verbal formulations is secondary and must
be understood to be grounded, to be validated, and to grow
out of faith in Christ.[2] I wrote a paperback on the subject a
few years ago,[3] and can here only indicate its conclusions in
the most summary fashion, in order to offer the reader a more
comprehensive picture of the subject-matter of this present
book. For fuller treatment I must refer to that earlier work.

The 'apostles', to use the term loosely to mean those who
first came to believe in Christ and to preach him, came to full
christian faith when they recognised God confronting them,
God communicating himself to them, in Christ. The Gospel
of John coming at the end of the apostolic age, shows a carefully thought out 'theology' or understanding of christian
faith precisely in these terms: it plays throughout on
the theme of 'seeing' merely materially and 'seeing spiritually'
(believing) with the true recognition or vision of faith; Philip
naïvely asks Jesus, 'Show us the Father and we ask no more',
and receives the reply, 'Anyone who has seen me has seen
the Father' (Jn 14: 8-9); the man born blind (Jn 9) is the type
of the gentiles, like those in John's Church at Ephesus, who

were born in darkness but came to true vision, whereas the leaders of the Jews, born within the mainstream of God's self-communication, end up blind; the climax of the Gospel is Thomas's profession of faith, 'My Lord and my God', which earns the reply, 'Blessed are those who have not seen (as eye-witnesses) but have believed (seen spiritually)' (Jn 20:29).[4]

Christ is God's 'last word', his ultimate self-expression and self-communication in human terms. It is not ultimately what Christ said or did that is God's self-communication, but he himself: he is the true bread from heaven that replaces the old manna (understood by the Jews as a symbol of the *Torah*); he is at once God's message and messenger, and it is only in recognising the messenger as God incarnate that the message is grasped, and the meaning seized, of what he said or did.

One can see at this point that 'faith' and 'revelation' are correlative terms. Revelation can be thought of as God's act of self-expression coming to its fullness in the incarnation. But until man grasps God so presenting himself, recognises him in his message and thereby begins to grasp the message – until, in fact, there is faith – no revelation to man has taken place.

In the case of the apostles, 'revelation received' is the total impact of Christ on these chosen witnesses. But he presented himself to them, not 'out of the blue' but born of a (Jewish) woman, born under the law, namely in the whole historical context of the revelation to Israel, as the centre and fulfilment of covenant, of prophecy, of promise, indeed of all Israel's aspirations. This will lead us below to consider more fully the process of revelation to Israel which culminates in Christ, and the fact that he was grasped by the apostles 'according to the scriptures'.

(b) *Our faith.*

There can really be no question of late generations, even those to whom the fourth gospel is addressed, sharing the faith of the apostles, unless they too truly encounter Christ and are able to recognise God addressing them in him. Hence the key to the faith of later generations, the key to our faith, is to be found in a thorough and radical grasp of the fact that the Church, the living People of God, is in truth the Body of Christ. The Risen Lord dwells in his People by the gift of his Spirit. It is there, where he is, in them, that men today are able to meet and recognise him.[5] In the case of the eye-witnesses themselves, it was not in their meeting with the mortal Jesus that christian faith came to birth, except in a preparatory, inchoate and defeated form: they all left him and ran away; the disciples on the road to Emmaus 'had been hoping' (Lk 24:21). Faith began in the encounter with and recognition of the Risen Christ, and the birth of the faith of the Church is signalised by Pentecost.[6] It is in his Spirit that the triumphant Lord is present and active in the group of his followers. It is among them that we are aware of and can respond to him. Hence it is that the message of the fourth gospel, the message of encouragement for those who have not seen but have believed, is valid for us today.

It is in the whole life of the whole People that Christ presents himself to us and calls for our response. He meets most of us first of all in our mothers and fathers, in our families, and then in a widening circle of deepening relation-ships. He meets us in the Church's saints, canonised and uncanonised: they reflect and express in different ways the endlessly unfolding richness of the presence and action of Christ in his Spirit in human history. He meets us in the liturgy and sacraments of the Church, in its tradition of scripture, its preaching and writing, its attitudes and mission to human society, its prayer, its silence.

Our faith, that is, our awareness of and response to Christ as he communicates himself to us, can be thought of as arising out of an interior and an exterior component. In the case of the apostles, the external factor is Christ encountered within the whole setting of Israel's history, scriptures, religion, aspira-tion. The interior factor is the gift of the Spirit to see truly and spiritually the meaning of all that Christ is and does and says. There were many who saw the evidence, materially, but did not believe – did not see with the eyes the Spirit gives.

John's gospel puts this in one way by saying 'No man can come to me unless he is drawn by the Father' (Jn 6: 44, 65). In the synoptic gospels Jesus' miracles are presented principally as 'powers', manifestations that it is God who is here at work heralding the last age and the conquest of evil. The fourth gospel develops the idea by portraying Jesus' 'works' both as the witness of the Father to Jesus, and as 'signs' which could only be read by those who, like the blind that Jesus cured, were given eyes to see: they were only truly signs to those who could see what they were signs of; others could even regard them as signs of the devil's work. Thus in christian tradition faith has been regarded as centrally a gift of God: not only does God give himself in Christ and his Spirit; but it is only in the gift of the Spirit that he can be recognised for who he is. It thus always remains a mystery of God's grace, ie of God's self-gift, why some believe and some do not. It was a bewildering problem to the earliest christian generations why the Jews still did not believe, and accounts for many strands in the New Testament documents. In writing to the Romans, Paul had his own solution: clearly God had allowed temporary blindness to the Jews, so that the Gospel should be preached to the gentiles; then, of course, the Jews too would believe: 'this partial blindness has come upon Israel only until the gentiles have been admitted in full strength; when that has happened, the whole of Israel will be saved' (Rom 11: 25-26). The tradition which framed Mark's gospel seems to argue that, if the Jews did not, and still do not, believe, then God could not have wanted them to; so Jesus spoke in parables precisely so that he should *not* be understood, except by the few chosen disciples (Mk 4: 11-12). The Church in which Matthew's gospel was formed is still wrestling with the problem and appealing somewhat desperately to the Jewish people over the heads of their leaders. By John's gospel it seems that hope is lost, and 'the Jews' are a symbol for resistance to the Gospel.

The separateness of what we have called the interior and exterior components of faith is clearest in the case of the gentiles or pagans to whom the Gospel was first preached, or in the case of pagan nations reached by later generations of

missionaries. To them, born 'blind' and outside the experience of God's revelation to Israel, Christ in his Church is
presented more wholly from the outside as external sign or
evidence. The first followers of Christ were Jews, and so the
interior action of the Spirit already took the form within their
experience of a sharing in and awareness of the religious heritage and expectation of Israel. In the modern western world
the non-believer or agnostic is, in spite of himself, heir to a
culture laced by centuries of christian belief; and so, in his
case, no very useful distinction can be made between the interior gift and action of the Spirit and the christian 'fact' as
external sign or evidence. In the case of the child born
of truly christian parents, external and internal realities
fuse into one: in a true sense the child is within the
Church from the outset, and baptism will bring fully
into the Church one who was never wholly outside it;
faith and the life of the Spirit are progressively mediated
to him by parents, family, the wider community of
believers; he grows within the faith of the Church.

(c) *The reasonableness of faith*

In this understanding of the matter, faith is self-authenticating. It is centrally a 'moment' (not necessarily a chronological moment) of recognition, but it deploys itself
progressively into a total response of the whole man.[7] Because
it is centrally a vision, an awareness, a recognition (of God communicating himself to me in Christ), it is open-eyed. Hence
it is inappropriate and misleading to speak of faith as 'a leap
in the dark', as is often done.[8] It could better be called, and is
at times experienced as, a leap into the light. However, here
we see darkly as in a reflection, and only in the Kingdom shall
we see face to face (1 Cor 13: 12): so a long and sound christian tradition speaks of the obscurity of faith's vision. We all
know very well from experience what that means: the 'vision'
comes and goes, and is at best a groping towards fullness.

Still, in considering the rationality or reasonableness of
faith it seems important, rather, to stress that it is a recognition, that we *do see*. Its reasonableness is inherent to itself. It

is reasonable, for it is the fullest response of the whole man, and therefore of his rational powers, to the most comprehensive reality; it is not reasoned, not the conclusion of an argument.[9] The power of the thinking Christian to relate his faith to his developing knowledge and understanding in other fields, and the power of the christian apologist to explain and defend faith in the face of the unending challenges that the development of thought and culture continually throws up, do not constitute the rationality of faith: they demonstrate anew, and indeed deepen, its inherent rationality.

In his book, *A History of Apologetics*,[10] Fr Avery Dulles traces with great thoroughness two constant strands in the christian effort, running through both catholic and protestant traditions, to relate faith to reason or to show that faith is reasonable. There is the 'extrinsic' strand that seeks to demonstrate or to establish the validity of christian faith from outside the experience itself. And there is the 'intrinsic' strand, clearly more favoured by Dulles himself, which asserts that faith is self-validating: even that it is in a sense circular, and necessarily elusive if not infuriating to the non-believer: when you see, you see. Given two such constant elements in human thinking from within the experience of christian faith, one is surely right to seek for complementary truths which they are expressing, rather than to take sides too exclusively for one or the other position.

It may be suggested that the 'extrinsic' tradition in apologetics is testifying to the continuity between christian and other human experience.[11] For in many if not all of his characteristically human activities (love, poetry, art, the pursuit of knowledge, hope and despair, being drawn to life or faced by death), particularly in his heights and in his depths, man is aware of a power of self-transcendence; in his very reaching out towards an absolute of some kind he is already dimly aware of it, he already half touches it by his groping, at least to the extent that to speak in terms of absolutes (freedom, justice, wisdom, love, peace) conveys meaning to him. Yet it cannot be argued that man's search and groping for an absolute, even his most profoundly

experienced need of it (as wholeness, fulfilment, etc), constitutes a proof that such an absolute exists. Revelation is an
act of God, not of man. Before a man can have faith (recognition), God must somehow act and present himself in answer
to man's searching. Faith is then man's response to the God
who so addresses him. But it is because man is already searching, already half aware, that he is able to recognise God when
he communicates himself.[12]

In these pages I have explicitly started from christian faith
and have purposely set it up as a norm and a fullness by
which we may try to understand other faiths, and various
dwindlings away of religious faith into twilight – and will
touch on this subject again. But in adopting this method,
which seems to me the proper one for a theologian, I do not
wish to suggest that God acts to reveal himself, and to bring
man to religious belief, only within christian experience: his
Spirit, which is in fact the Spirit of Christ even when not
recognised as such, 'has filled the earth' and reaches all men;
Christ is the real light which enlightens every man. But our
understanding of faith precisely as resulting from man's recognition of *God's* self-communication excludes the possibility
of man passing over to it and reaching it simply out of his
own inner human resources and effort, precisely as human
and originating from himself. Wherever in human records
there is evidence of belief in God, it is testimony to an awareness of God's action. The arguments of 'extrinsecist' apologists
display precisely the human factors upon which God works,
the human groping which God comes to meet; in so far as
they take their stance outside specifically religious experience
or awareness of God, and work simply from there, they are
not capable thereby of reaching the God who presents himself
to faith.

Hence it may be suggested that the 'intrinsic' tradition of
apologetics testifies to the radical discontinuity between
christian faith and all other human experience, even the
religious awareness of Judaism. This discontinuity stems from
the unique fact of the incarnation, the self-expression and
self-communication of God in his becoming flesh. Here, even
if nowhere else, we may speak of an 'intervention' of God

in history, whereby he openly and fully presents himself to man for man's recognition.

The christian thinker or theologian thus remains somewhat ill at ease in the uncertain area between philosophy and theology designated as philosophy of religion. The philosopher as such cannot validate (or invalidate) religious belief; he may construct arguments leading towards, and perhaps reaching, an abstract God. He will have difficulty, as philosopher, in allowing validity to such terms as 'awareness' of God, 'experience' of God. He will necessarily produce many critiques, from an 'outside' standpoint, of religious language in general. The christian thinker in turn cannot validate from outside itself the experience of encountering the living God in Christ. And yet he must lay claim to such terms as 'experience', 'awareness', 'recognition' of God, as this is precisely what is centrally constitutive of christian faith.

Man's awareness of God in Christ, with its potentially total response absorbing the whole of man's being and life, is in traditional terms a 'virtue', capable of being present more or less, capable of indefinite growth. Thus we should not place a further radical break or discontinuity between the widely shared experience of christian faith and its more occasional flowering in the graces of mystical prayer. Rather, the clear testimony of the mystics that they have direct and clear experience of God should be seen as throwing light on the more diffused, uncrystallised, less explicit awareness of God's self-giving that is the core of 'ordinary' faith, and ordinary prayer. The classic, even technical, definition of mystical prayer (whether sporadic or continuous) is the direct experience of God within the soul. All faith is an awareness of being forestalled and confronted by God's initiative – not, as we have tried to show, the product of man's effort. What is so specific to mystical prayer as to point to a discontinuity between it and ordinary prayer or faith, is: not the element of being aware of God in a personal encounter, which can be seen to be simply heightened as between ordinary and extraordinary prayer; but the awareness of God within the soul, not so much as an object but almost as a subject taking charge. This fullest development of the life of faith known to christian experience can help us to see what is centrally constitutive of that life in its more rudimentary or initial stages. It enables us to focus the fact that, centrally, faith is an awareness or recognition of God's action, not ours. This is why it is self-validating. This is why it is reasonable. This is why it always remains something of a mystery, something of a charmed circle – like falling in love – which cannot simply be made available to others by explanation or persuasion.

(d) *Faith and doctrines*[13]

I have argued that faith is primarily in Christ as we encounter him in his Church, and that it is a response of the whole man. Using Paul's word 'obedience' in his sense of a hearing that is also a heeding, Vatican II in its *Constitution on Divine Revelation* (5) speaks of faith as 'an obedience by which man entrusts his whole self freely to God'. But because faith is a response of the whole man, an intellectual or conceptual element is present from the beginning. Faith does not exist in a 'pure' state or form, as a direct inter-personal recognition in no way formulated or conceptualised by the believer. It is only in the act of expressing reality in mental patterns of some kind that man invests reality with meanings, grasps its meanings.

The conceptual element may begin by being very rudimentary and pictorial. Thomas's confession of faith, 'My Lord and my God', is already conceptualised, though simply. We might well wonder what he meant by 'Lord' (*kyrios*); whether he understood that Jesus had always been God, indeed had as God pre-existed the incarnation (as John's gospel certainly understands); whether he had any clear idea of the Son as distinct from the Father though equal to him, etc. These are, of course, precisely the questions that subsequent generations put to the apostolic witness.

Hence 'faith' does not chronologically precede 'doctrine', though it overflows doctrine and grounds it. 'Doctrine' means teaching: it must be understood as a conceptual and verbal element that is there from the beginning of faith; a grasp of meaning for oneself which can then become an expression to others of meaning and of conviction. It is an element of faith that is capable of, and indeed requires, development in various ways. John records that Our Lord promised to send his Spirit to guide the apostles into all truth, to unfold himself to them (Jn 16: 13-15). So the Church throughout its life, and each of us throughout our own, can continue to deploy 'the inexhaustible riches of Christ' into more full and diversified expression.

But man does not express himself solely in words, still less solely in words that correspond to abstract thought. The Church expresses her whole grasp of Christ in a whole life, which includes the cultural forms of poetry, music, dancing, art, architecture, in or out of liturgical settings; and of course she also expresses it in whole areas of behaviour towards human beings and human society. Indeed, in her *doctrina* or teaching she makes use of all these forms of expression. Hence theology, or the attempt at precise verbal formulation of the meaning of Christ, does not exist in isolation but in a whole christian life. Indeed, the life must come first, and theology can only be the expression of an existing experience. Doctrines (in the plural) cannot develop by a merely cerebral-verbal detached process that is self-propelled.

Consequently, to believe in what the Church teaches is not a matter of mental assent to doctrines proposed by others, by 'them'. It is first and foremost to encounter Christ in the christian people and to share in the christian experience. Then the Church's doctrines can be recognised as a true formulation of what is our own experience.

Doctrines develop because the christian experience itself develops. The first band of believers in the Risen Christ had very limited cultural, spatial and temporal horizons, as they looked to a speedy Second Coming and consummation. The Church of Jerusalem moved out in time into a gentile mission; from one small community to a scattered group of larger communities. This was one radical alteration of the christian experience, which brought new questions of church–church and church–world relationship, new questions of inner life and organisation. Above all the Church moved from a mainly Jewish culture into a mainly Hellenised one, and had positively to translate its self-expression into different cultural forms; it came in time to face questions posed by a Greek philosophical way of analysing reality and meaning which would never have occurred to a Jew of Palestine. And so the process has gone on ever since. Because the People is firmly and wholly in history, the christian experience undergoes constant development. So, therefore, does the doctrinal expression of this experience.

(e) *Unity in faith*

Once it is recognised that faith is given to Christ encountered in a historically and culturally conditioned Church, it has also to be recognised that unity or disunity in faith cannot simply be equated with unity or disunity in doctrine. Indeed, it becomes something of a problem to know what exactly is meant by disunity in faith. How do you know when Christians are united or disunited in faith? What are the criteria for deciding such a question?

Clearly, if some conceptual grasp and expression goes with every act or experience of faith, then at least in what is felt to be most global and basic one may be certain that there is agreement or disagreement in faith. If a man will not admit that the man Jesus was and is divine, both God and man, then I am quite clear that we disagree in faith: I would be prepared to say he has not got specifically christian faith, and is not what I mean by a Christian. But if he does assent to that, and it clearly means very much to him, and yet rejects further doctrinal elaborations that I would regard as essential to a christian creed, I become uncertain what is the appropriate language to use. We are not wholly divided in faith; indeed, he has what is basic and essential, from which the rest develops. Are we united in faith, but divided in doctrine? Or are we basically united but at the same time also divided in faith? Most would probably opt for the latter statement. But once you go beyond an agreed root, which might be described as the recognition of God communicating himself to me in Christ, and add doctrines that are also considered essential to unity in faith, you run into a double difficulty. The first is that there seems no point in any full list or explanation of christian doctrines where one can draw a line between the essential and the inessential: have doctrines which have been authoritatively defined in the course of time become essential, whereas they were previously inessential, for unity *in faith*? Can it be that the fruitful classification of christian experience should imperil and even destroy the unity of Christians in faith? The second difficulty is that the more elaborately your doctrines are worked out, the more you are running into the cultural conditioning and limitations of all human statements, and so the less certain it becomes that men are really disagreeing, or are progressively ceasing to communicate, to understand each other. More basic still, you are running into the increasing cultural conditioning of the actual christian experience itself, which doctrinal statements attempt to express.

At least we need to recognise that, if the main christian bodies all accept creeds like the Apostles' Creed and the Nicaeo-Constantinopolitan Creed, they have already a massive and fundamental unity in faith that precedes and underlies their divisions. They are basically one, not wholly divided. And this is because their root unity is one that Christ himself gives them. They soon come to experience it when they cease to live at arm's length and increasingly begin to share each other's christian lives.

However, there are many other aspects to unity in faith apart from the doctrinal one, and in pursuing these reflections we have been in danger of ignoring the warning given at the end of the last section. Doctrine does not develop simply interiorly and on its own by an intellectual process, but is an expression of a whole christian experience. And faith, even if it always contains an intellectual or conceptual element, is not simply an intellectual assent to Christ. It is a response of the whole man, discovered, developed, and shared in a christian community. Further, the whole of christian life is an expression of faith, its worship and spirituality, its concern for others, its sense of mission. Consequently a doctrinal criterion of unity is not sufficient, even if necessary. There is, for instance, point in the protest of groups of Christians belonging to different Churches and engaged together in some work of charity and apostolate, when they say: 'You theologians simply sustain and propagate division. What we are doing is what christianity is really about. We *are* united in faith.' There is point in the protest, even if we cannot accept that such christian living is itself the whole criterion of unity in faith. It is certainly not irrelevant.

Hence a paradox. So far from unity in faith being something that christian bodies must achieve before they can unite, one must ask whether they can have unity in faith until they have united. Unity in faith must first be a shared community experience before it can express itself in common doctrinal formulas. One notices that Catholics (for example) can disagree and argue with each other about forms of expression of even central doctrines without doubting that they have unity in faith. They are sure of this because they live and work together in one Church, pray together, receive Communion together (without, incidentally, being called on to make any profession of faith before being admitted to Communion).

Indeed, can christian bodies in a real and full sense have unity in doctrine before they unite? They may hammer out long formulas of agreement, as so many union schemes have done, but is this more than notional or conceptual unity, as long as it is not an expression of shared christian experience?

Our own time has come to recognise far more clearly the function of language, not as a direct mirror of reality, but as shared symbols of experience. It has come to see that all language is culturally and historically conditioned, and belongs within a whole complex of cultural attitudes, within and by reference to which it has its meaning. Hence neat systems of philosophy are suspect, not for what clarification they are able to give, but for their tendency to be exclusive and to be blind to, or openly to reject, other ways of expressing meaning. With any pluralism of philosophy there necessarily goes a pluralism of theologies, or in theology, ie in the conceptual expression of the experience of faith. This

adds an important dimension to christian struggles for unification. We would happily unite, if only we were convinced
that we shared the same faith – ie were already united! It
seems, rather, that in the process of unification there will
come a point where there is a gap to be jumped. All has been
done that is humanly possible to ensure in advance that, on
uniting, unity in faith will be experienced. But it can only
be creatively experienced by in fact uniting.

One factor contributing very greatly to unity, because
already an emerging experience of existing unity, is the actual
dialogue (at whatever level) between ecclesially divided
Christians. The whole process, which has already become
world-wide, is progressively establishing a communion of
thought. This is a hard thing, perhaps an impossible thing,
to define: once more, it is something that is first experienced:
and perhaps it can only be experienced by involvement, and
not conveyed secondhand. It is quite different from agreement in doctrine, in the traditional sense of acceptance
of the same formulas. Rather is it a growing understanding of
legitimate differences of aspect and of emphasis, and hence of
differences in doctrine, held together within a shared experience of communication. It is not different in principle
from the process that can be seen to have taken place at
Vatican II: documents like *Lumen Gentium* are evidence,
not of single-minded uniformity, but of an unfinished
dialogue, indicating many pulls in different directions, and
resulting either in compromise formulas or in the laying side
by side of formulas in tension – all within the experience of
one faith. One sign of this communion of thought is that
avowed Catholics and Protestants, who have got to know each
other in theological discussion, often feel they have intellectually or theologically far more in common with each other
than they have with some members of their own Churches.
They progressively come to realise that they are not in fact
divided in christian faith in any significant sense.

Anglican and Protestant Churches in hammering out
schemes for union have sometimes reached a compromise
formula on doctrinal questions, which has satisfied a central
majority, but has raised objections from left and right. Some-

times they have more straightforwardly stated where they agree and where they at present differ. Catholics, too, are painfully learning to disagree with each other instead of speaking in choral unison. (Professional theologians have, of course, always enjoyed a fair measure of disagreement!) One may, therefore, tentatively suggest that christian thinkers in the ecumenical field generally have moved into a new stage. The first stage was the simple laying side by side of confessional differences – taking an honest look at each other. The second stage was the struggle to reach agreed statements through protracted dialogue. Now, as much by personal contact as by formal statement, a communion of thought is being achieved capable of holding some differences together within itself. In such a situation it seems possible to envisage that Churches may find they can unite on the basis of a minimum, rather than a maximum, of actual credal or confessional statement. In the history of creeds and councils it has been the characteristic aim formally to define only the minimum necessary for the unity and mission of the Church. For the unity: we have learnt that this is not the same as uniformity, that catholicity includes welcome for all cultural expressions of christian faith; and yet the Church can only have a sense of identity as Christ's body if she gives expression to what she receives from him. For the mission: it is not the task of the Church to live in mutual admiration, but to preach to the world what she receives from Christ. The two purposes coincide, in that the christian people can only fulfil its calling, if it can speak one gospel to the world, and be heard as one voice. If over the centuries the human grasp of Christ in his body has become richer and more diverse, as the Church has entered new cultures, new historical situations, new developments and differentiations of human learning itself, we should nevertheless reflect very deeply on what is happening when we demand 'more doctrine' from our contemporaries before communion with them than did Peter on the day of Pentecost, or the apostolic or patristic age as it carried the gospel to the ends of the earth. The progressive reaching out of the Church in the ways indicated is a fulfilment of her apostolic mission. Must it necessarily imperil and weaken her unity?

Hence one may tentatively suggest that the criteria for unity in faith are complex and cannot simply be reduced to one. They have, rather, to be lived in creative tension. Roughly they might be summarised under three heads: that agreement on central doctrinal formulation which is felt to constitute the essential Gospel to the world; a common involvement, in response to God's love, in worship of him and in service of man; an acceptance of such diversity and emphasis in these areas of doctrine, worship and mission as the experience of unity is able to sustain. Orthodoxy, orthopraxy, catholicity.

NOTES

1. Roger Aubert, *Le Problème de l'Acte de Foi*, University of Louvain, 2nd ed., 1950, is the classic exposition of this stage of the debate.

2. The chapter 'Christian Faith as Personal Response', by James P. Mackey in *Faith: its nature and meaning*, ed. Paul Surlis, Dublin, Gill and Macmillan, 1972, sets this theological development in perspective.

3. John Coventry, sj, *The Theology of Faith*, Cork, The Mercier Press, 1968. Chapter I, 'Outline', gives the gist of the matter.

4. Cf *The Theology of Faith*, pp 26-8, which draw heavily on an article, 'Eiden Kai Episteusen', by Oscar Cullmann, in *Aux Sources de la Tradition Chrétienne:* Mélanges offerts à M. Maurice Goguel, Neuchatel and Paris, Delachaux et Niestlé, 1950.

5. See E. Schillebeeckx, *Christ: the sacrament of encounter with God*, London, Sheed and Ward, 1963.

6. See more fully in Chapter III, section (b), below.

7. Cf *The Theology of Faith*, pp 15-16.

8. The phrase and its associated way of thinking has various origins: partly the propositional view of faith which is in difficulties to justify intellectual assent to mysteries; partly the emotional or anti-intellectualist flavour attached to the word 'faith' by idealist philosophers and theologians.

9. See *The Theology of Faith*, chapters 4 and 5.

10. London, Hutchinson, 1971.

11. Professor Pannenberg is today the chief exponent of the view, in reaction against Barth, that it can be *shown* that history reveals God.

12. For further discussion of this question in another context, see Chapter 4, section (b), below.

13. I have published the material of this and the next section in an article, 'Faith and Doctrines', in *The Furrow*, March 1973,

Chapter Two

REVELATION AND THE OLD TESTAMENT

It has already been seen that faith and revelation are correlative concepts: 'revelation' primarily emphasises God's action and self-communication, 'faith' regards man's response. But no revelation has in fact taken place until it has been met by faith: God has not disclosed or given himself to man until man receives the gift. In this chapter and the next I wish to examine in more detail the process by which God reveals himself and man recognises God. For the sake of clarity I will use the term 'Israel' to designate the People who produced the Book, and 'Old Testament' and 'New Testatment' for the Book(s). Hence it will be seen from its title that this chapter wishes to examine the process of revelation to Israel and the relationship of the Book to that process.

(a) *What is the Old Testament?*

It has rightly been remarked that the Old Testament is more a library than a book. It covers a vast span of time and of religious and cultural development. It includes greatly differing types of literature: for example, doctrine, law, history, poetry, fiction, political pamphleteering.

The Old Testament is the chief written witness to the religious experience of Israel over some 1,700 years or more. Israel and its religious awareness comes first. Any idea of 'inspiration' must first apply to the People: it is in or upon them that the Spirit of God acts, producing a growing awareness of him. Much has recently been written on the idea of biblical inspiration.[1] The traditional christian doctrine is that the Book, this particular verbal expression of Israel's religious experience, is guided or selected by God. I would like to suggest that what is central (and sufficient) to secure this idea, and what accords with what we know of the formation of the Old Testament as we now have it, is a process of selection carried out by Israel itself. The religious consciousness of Israel progressively selected *this* writing, in *this* form, as truly reflecting its faith – modifying some of it in the process, jettisoning other forms. For instance, how is a true prophet (in the sense of a 'speaker for God' and not just a predicter of future events) distinguished from a false prophet? Surely by the religious consciousness of the people being able, then or later, to say, 'Yes, this truly expresses our faith'. The classical prophets have been called the conscience of Israel: they spoke for and to it, and thus were remembered and revered as true prophets. So it is basically the People which is the 'carrier' of inspiration, because the vehicle of the Spirit. The idea does not exclude that of God specially calling an individual and making him aware of something that needs saying in the name of God to the People (Israel or the Church), but the prophet only becomes a prophet when he is known as one; no revelation without faith. It is the People's faith which 'canonises' this writing rather than that, and which continues to nourish its own faith by constant reflection on writings which are seen in different ways to express the heart of its religious experience. The process is quite simply analogous to that by which, in the secular sphere, a piece of writing or an author becomes a classic. Shakespeare became a classic because the people saw his works as expressing, capturing, immortalising in a unique way the cultural values of an age; the people continues to treasure this expression and to nourish its later cultural development on it.

The Old Testament is only one witness to the religious inspiration of Israel. The Book does not exist apart from the cult, just as christian doctrine does not exist apart from christian life or have meaning except as an expression of it.

There are two further facts to notice about the Old Testament in this context. The first is that Israel kept adding to it, century after century, until at least some 150 years before Christ. The second is that much of the Old Testament, as we now have it, is the result of constant re-editing, re-writing, re-formulation, of older material. One has only to instance the discoverable sources of the hexateuch, the identification of the characteristic deuteronomic theology and view of history, the growth of 'the book' of Isaiah. Again, if one takes any theological theme such as creation, or the idea of sin, or of personal responsibility, one can trace a development of religious and spiritual awareness in the course of Israel's history that is reflected in strata of our present Old Testament 'books'. Indeed, the covenant theology of the deuteronomic school entails the idea of future fulfilment opening out into further promise.

It would appear to follow from these facts that the Old Testament was not regarded as 'sacred scripture', as the definitive and fixed holy writing that expressed God's message, by Israel itself, ie by the People who wrote it and accepted it. Later parts of the Old Testament never quote earlier parts as holy scripture, though they sometimes use earlier parts. The idea of 'holy scripture' was not an idea of the People at the time of their writing it. It became their idea later, namely in the inter-testamental period, and one may pause to wonder why Christians adopted this idea, which was a product of the rabbinic schools.[2] Historically speaking the reason is, of course, quite simply that Jesus and his followers were born into the time of inter-testamental Judaism, and not into the time of the Israel that produced the Old Testament, and accepted the ideas of their time.

For the moment we may leave aside the theological question involved here, and consider another.[3] Rabbinic Judaism is a development, a prolongation, of elements to be found in the Old Testament, and to that extent carries on the 'development of doctrine' that took place in Israel and is witnessed to by the Old Testament itself. But at the same time this period gives totally new emphases and directions to themes which are not particularly characteristic of the Old Testament: notably messianism, apocalyptic and eschatological reference, legalistic emphasis. So the question arises: if we regard Israel as the vehicle of inspiration (ie of the Spirit) in producing the Old Testament, why do we not regard them as inspired in producing rabbinic Judaism and its writings? The answer can be drawn from what has already been said about the process of recognition and canonisation of the Old Testament. We do in fact regard rabbinic Judaism as inspired, not directly in its writings, but precisely and only in so far as its main themes are taken up in, and find their expression and fulfilment in, the preaching of the Gospel. It is the 'New' Israel (or true Israel), the christian People, the full vehicle of the Spirit, that is led to select and to reject from the characteristic thought-forms and verbal expressions of rabbinic Judaism. It is the Church's discernment that decides what in the inter-testamental period is a true or valid development, and what is of less or of no worth. Its criterion for doing so will be considered in the next chapter.

(b) *History and revelation in Israel*

Israel had no word for 'revelation', no concept of revelation: they had a view of history. To Israel, God was Lord of history. They moved in the course of time from the conviction that Yahweh guided their history to the conviction that he guided all history. This is their idea of God as creator: the opening chapters of Genesis are not a view of the origins of the universe arising out of cosmological curiosity, but a view of God's planning of the history of peoples and special choice among them of Israel.[4]

Israel's awareness of God, belief in God, is simply a datum: there is no evidence of its being arrived at (which, of course, is equally true of all other peoples). They have no 'concept of God' in a hellenic sense, but a given awareness of God which they progressively and variously conceptualise. Their awareness of God as directing their history develops eventually (about the seventh century) into the full covenant theology of our present Old Testament. They were convinced that God had intervened notably at specific points in their history, and so had changed the course of events; but also that he had charge of it all the time. They saw things happening to them because they had been faithful or unfaithful to God: for instance, in our Bible the history of the kingly period leading to the exile is written in this vein. But their view of history, unlike that of other ancient peoples, always looked to the future. However unfaithful they might be, God would not finally be unfaithful to them or to his own promise. Their faith is a hope–faith, a reliance on God's love (and the word 'faith' in the New Testament continues to carry this overtone). Their understanding of God was never simply a matter of interpreting past history in theological terms.

Clearly Israel was convinced that God intervened in 'outside' events. The christian thinker must, then, ask: Did he? Is it somehow part of our faith to think that he did? Is our belief in and understanding of revelation tied up with the idea?

One solution to this question has been given in terms of 'salvation history' (*Heilsgeschichte*). The idea was launched by Oscar Cullman,[5] and appears to be made up basically of three assertions: that God guides history all the time, so that in a broad sense all history is salvation history; that God intervenes notably at special and separated points, which themselves constitute salvation history in the more specific sense; that these interventions enable man to recognise God's control all the time.

The idea caught on for a time in the theological scene (and was perhaps over-hastily adopted at points by Vatican II), because it high-lighted the fact that, for Israel, history was the vehicle of revelation; that Israel discerned God, not (Moses apart) in epiphanies, but in their own developing historical experience. It has, however, come under considerable criticism, for four reasons in particular. First, the theory suggests that there are two sorts of event, sacred and secular, and not just two sorts of interpretation of one kind of event. Secondly, it either suggests that salvation history is a matter of disconnected leaps and bounds; or, in its broader assertion that all history is salvific, it is ambiguous as to why some events are selected as more saving than others. Thirdly, many theologians are profoundly ill at ease with any idea of God's 'intervening' in history, in the sense of changing the course of events, or making things happen which observable human processes would not have brought about anyway. Fourthly, and this is connected with the previous point, the theory seems to picture God as 'outside' history, whereas he could just as well be said to be 'inside' it; as a purely transcendent and 'supra-natural' God, who does not leave his creation to function in the way he made it; as a God who appears to achieve his purposes only by repeated interventions at our level.

I would suggest that the only tenable resolution of this question must be along the following lines:

(1) There are no interventions or 'acts of God' in the history of Israel, in the sense of events not explicable by the secular historian. But of course, as we shall consider more fully in a moment, the secular historian must operate within categories proper to secular history. The suggestion will be that there are futher dimensions of meaning open to discovery in secular events.

(2) The 'locus' of revelation in Israel's history was solely the religious consciousness of Israel: in their minds (in the broad sense of their human appreciation) and not in particular outside events. By this is meant, not that God existed solely in their minds, but that God's Spirit acted in or on their minds to discern him in events otherwise secular. In other words, the 'locus' of revelation (God's self-communicating action), though not of God himself, was solely the religious consciousness of Israel. It was Israel that was inspired, or inspirited, and not the Red Sea. Hence we should read their poetic narrative about 'the wonderful works of God' as a witness to their own vivid and in many ways unique sense of God, and see the special action of God in this alone. (It was, and still is, their religion that made their history, and not vice versa.) Recorded history is recorded human experience, and not some mechanical recording of merely physical sequences untouched by human awareness. To Israel, human experience was religious, and their record of it was theological. This was not just part of its meaning to them, but their comprehensive category of meaning.

(3) Israel certainly believed that God had specially acted

'out there' in the Exodus, etc. We should perhaps interpret this conviction as eschatological, as having a meaning that Israel could not itself discern, as pointing forward to and expressing hope of the one and only time that God can be truly said to have intervened in history – namely, in his becoming man in Jesus Christ.

This, I suggest, is a quite coherent and defensible position for a christian theologian. But it no doubt leaves some questions unanswered. Is the Old Testament, then, to be thought of as history? Is it true history or is it false? And, to a christian theologian, does it matter?[6]

Philosophers of history can now be said to be generally agreed that all historical writing is interpretation. It necessarily selects its 'facts'. At different points of time history puts different questions to man's past, and the viewpoint of the question determines the type of answer (which is why it continually has to be rewritten). The positivist view or ideal of historical writing has generally been abandoned. Historical questioning and writing is about human experience, not about merely physical, 'out-there', wholly objective events (untouched by human hands), which a properly trained mind would need only to photograph. If the shape of Cleopatra's nose altered the shape of the world, this is because it affected Caesar and Antony. What Cleopatra normally had for breakfast did not (as far as we know), and is therefore not a historical fact or event.

History-enquiry cannot be defined in secular or philosophical terms in such a way as to exclude *a priori* the discovery of God in everyday human experience, or in the heights and depths of human experience. But nor can any secular view or horizon of history as enquiry support the idea of discovering God in historical experience. If revelation and faith are correlative, there remains a fundamental, but not vicious, circularity. Only to faith are historical events revelation. Whatever events may have occurred, with whatever effects on human beings, they remain events which the secular historian as such must seek to, and must claim to be in principle able to, explain by his normal processes and within his secular horizon. The believer cannot maintain that they prove God's action or guidance, within that horizon. It was said just above, in passing, that Jewish belief made Israel's history – which is true to a lesser extent of the religion of all peoples. This *is* a proper subject-matter for the secular historian. The validity of the beliefs, in their specifically religious content, is not.

But is the Old Testament, then, real or true history? Well, it is obviously not modern history, but it is not for that reason simply 'not history' but something else. Modern history could only grow out of more elementary or rudimentary history, just as modern science only grew out of earlier philosophies of nature. And it must be realised that all early history, not just that of Israel, is theological: it colours its memories by religious conviction. The myths of Hercules, which are Dorian in origin, when coupled with archaeological excavations, notably of pottery, enable the modern historian to trace the route actually followed by the Dorian Greeks in their invasion of Greece in the tenth century BC, from the north via Thessaly and Argos to the Peloponnese: embedded in the myth is the historical memory of the invading peoples. Similarly the hexateuch enables the modern historian to get some idea of the eventual coalescence of various cognate peoples into Israel in the Promised Land. So of course the Old Testament is history; not our kind of history, but capable of yielding hard evidence for the modern historian. In this respect, it is no different in principle from Herodotus.

What, then, is the Old Testament? It is the surviving written witness of those who eventually formed one people with one religion, Israel, to the process of revelation: ie to their grasp of God, under the action of his Spirit, as the ultimate meaning of their recorded memories. It is a classic by any criterion. But the Old Testament is not itself revelation nor is revelation 'contained' in it simply as a series of doctrines or propositions. The locus of revelation is the religious consciousness of Israel. Revelation is a process. It is the action of God's Spirit on the spirit of man, enabling him to grasp God as the ultimate meaning of human experience. The Old Testament is Israel's verbal witness to this meaning.

(c) *Revelation in creation*

An older theology, with a distinction between nature and grace understood as a distinction between classes of men, had a problem here. Christians, and by extension Israel, were seen to be in receipt of the grace of Christ and so in a supernatural order; others in the merely natural order. Clearly, man can come to know God through creation, and has always done so; but this could not be relevant to salvation, which comes only through the grace of Christ. If it could come some other way, then the incarnation and the redemptive work of Christ would appear to be unnecessary. Hence other religions were regarded as at best irrelevant (natural religion, natural mysticism, etc) and at worst demonic.

But this does not square with Romans 1: 18 ff. If men are 'inexcusable', and God has given them up to their depraved reason, then presumably they could have reached salvation and not been abandoned by God. Nor does it square with the universalist theme of Old and New Testaments, which underlies Romans and is explicit in 1 Tim 2: 4: 'God our saviour, who desires all men to be saved and to come to knowledge of the truth.' So the problem for such a theory is how the grace of Christ can reach men, even those who lived before his time, by their contemplating nature.

It has first to be observed that any revelation in creation would still be revelation in history, because nature can only reveal God in so far as it makes an impact on man; it would still be revelation in human experience of life, and not just some non-human message written in the stars and mountains. And, of course, nature includes man himself – oneself and others. So the question becomes how we are to understand man-in-the-world's self-understanding as a vehicle of revelation in a relevant sense.

Briefly, a modern theory of grace, whether or not assisted by such perspectives as those of Teilhard de Chardin, understands that God did not 'first' create and 'then' adopt the plan of sharing his life with men through Christ. The biblical view is that he created for Christ,[7] and that the Spirit who stirs all men is always the Spirit of Christ, Professor Pannenberg, basing himself on Tillich and Teilhard de Chardin, has a particular development of this theme.[8] In Old and New Testaments, he asserts, the Spirit is God's gift of life – of all life – and so is universal in human experience. Christian awareness is a particularly clear manifestation, consciousness, interpretation, of what is common to all men. Men are specifically human, spiritual, precisely and only because God draws them ever forward into his own life by the gift of his Spirit. Christian revelation alone manifests what is the nature of the force that draws all men, namely the Spirit sent through the Risen Christ. So revelation to Israel is a growing manifestation and interpretation of all human experience in terms of God's gift of his Spirit, which reaches its fullness in Christ. Indeed, it is only looking back, as it were, from Christ that the Old Testament's 'true' meaning can be discerned, as he is the fulfilment of its promise.

It is true that no one comes to Christ unless the Father draws him. But the fourth gospel did not fully grasp that he draws all men to Christ, even if not to an explicit recognition of him or an explicit understanding of the force that is drawing them. In this perspective, all human awareness of God is at least inchoate awareness of Christ, and is of a piece with Judaeo-Christian revelation and religion, which is the central 'locus' in history, so we believe, of man's religious awareness. Hence all history is revelation in the same sense, and not in two radically different senses, natural and supernatural. This, of course, is not to deny the uniqueness of Christ, which rests on the incarnation; rather is it to emphasise his centrality in history. Neither is it to deny or blur the distinction between the natural and the supernatural: nature is not one class of men as distinct from others; nor is it one separable element in human experience; it is the created material on which God works, which he transforms, to which he communicates himself.

This view justifies starting our treatment of faith with christian faith, rather than with the general human phenomenon of religious belief. One sees more clearly in the centre of the stage, where the spotlight falls, while light shades off into darkness in the wings. But because all human experience (history) is revelation of Christ, then all response to God, all faith, is of a piece with christian faith. Yet, as was observed above, while there is continuity there is also a discontinuity between christian faith and all other religious awareness: recognition that God became a man, and a recognition of God addressing us person-to-person in him, is totally transforming, totally and radically new.

NOTES

1. For a thorough survey see B. Vawter, *Biblical Inspiration*, London, Hutchinson, 1972.
2. For this whole question see C. F. Evans, *Is 'Holy Scripture' Christian?* (and other essays), London, SCM, 1971; and N. Lohfink, *The Christian Meaning of the Old Testament*, London, Burns and Oates, 1969.
3. Cf J. Barr, *Old and New in Interpretation*, London, SCM, 1966.
4. See R. Butterworth, *The Theology of Creation*, Cork, The Mercier Press, 1969.
5. See, for instance, O. Cullmann, *Salvation in History*, London. SCM, 1967, where he answers critics of his earlier writings on this theme.
6. These questions are tackled by Alan Richardson, *History Sacred and Profane*, London, SCM, 1964. Though illuminating about the positivist ideal of history, he leaves the reader hesitant about acts of God in history.
7. See more fully R. Butterworth, op. cit., pp 71-90; and H Küng, *Justification*, London, Burns Oates, 1966, pp. 120ff.
8. A first sketch appeared in Pannenberg's chapter in *Spirit, Faith and Church* (ed. Pannenberg, Dulles, Braaten, Philadelphia, Westminster Press, 1970), and a fuller version in *Theology*, January 1972.

Chapter Three

REVELATION AND THE NEW TESTAMENT

(a) *The consciousness of Christ*

If I may dare to say it once more, whatever process of self-communication God adopts, no revelation in fact takes place until it is received by man. God chose to express himself fully and finally in human terms by becoming man, by becoming *a* man, within the mortal conditions of human history. The Word (God's self-expression) became flesh. So the central 'place' or locus of revelation, central both in terms of God acting to communicate himself and of man receiving and grasping this self-communication of God, is the consciousness of Christ.[1]

In view of the centuries in which, in opposition to the Arianism of large areas of the Empire, the Church found it necessary to stress the divinity of Jesus almost to the point of obscuring his humanity, it is probably still necessary to say something about the true Chalcedonian model in christology. The humanity of Jesus is the humanity of the Second Person of the Trinity, the humanity of the Word. The Word is divine, and so has the 'knowledge' or 'consciousness' of God (one knows the words are never quite appropriate, but they are the best we have). We must first *think* the divine and human knowledge of Christ as quite separate, and out of communication with each other, because the former is un-created and divine, the latter created and human, before we can begin to consider and try to understand some kind of (created) effect within the human consciousness, as a result of the co-existence of divine and human 'mind' in one (divine) Person. The divine omniscience cannot simply be 'poured just as it is' into the human consciousness, because the latter is totally incapable of receiving it. So, for any (created) mystical or infused awareness of God and God's will in the mind of the mortal Jesus, we have to be guided by the evidence, not by any reverential and misplaced impulse to maximise: this would not truly glorify Jesus, but on the contrary minimise and endanger his true humanity. He was born a true baby, with a baby's consciousness, and died a man of his time. There must have been a growing grasp by him of God's saving action through him. 'As Jesus grew up, he advanced in wisdom and in favour with God and man' (Lk 2:52). 'Ours is not a high priest unable to sympathise with our weaknesses, but one who has been tested in every way, as we are, only without sin' (Heb 4:15). So we not only can but must accept that Jesus' awareness of his Father (Lk 2:9), of his Father's will for man, of his own role in that design, was not fully there from the beginning of his life, grew in the course of his life, and was still fully human at the end of it. There is no theological objection, or objection in principle, to our supposing, for example, that the mortal Jesus, while preaching that God's Rule (kingship) was present among Israel in himself in a definitive way, also preached a final Realm (kingdom) of God as coming imminently; and so had no clear idea of a time, let alone a very long time, intervening between his own earthly end and the end of the ages; and so, in his mortal life, had no clear idea of the Church as a body of believers continuing in history after his death.

For it was not the mortal Jesus who founded the Church, but the Risen Christ.

And here a further point must be made. However fully there developed in the mind of Jesus a grasp of God's self-gift to man through his own (Jesus') humanity, we can and must make a clear distinction between the servant state of the mortal Jesus and the glorified state of the Risen Lord. We have not got the biographical material to trace the growth of awareness of the mortal Jesus. But this central process of revelation is only completed in the Risen Christ. We must not make the mistake that devotional literature has often made of assigning the attributes and qualities of the glorified manhood of the Risen Christ to the mortal state of Jesus, who was

truly a man like us, born of a woman, born under the Law.
'Faith' is perhaps not an appropriate word to designate the
human grasp by Jesus of God's self-communication in himself. And this because his human nature *is* the humanity of
the Second Person: it is hypostatically united to the Word of
God, and ours is not; there is therefore a radical difference
between his grasp and ours. In our case, dawning faith is
dawning recognition of Another addressing me. In Jesus' case
is is more a growth of self-awareness from within. The only
available clue in christian experience is the 'infused knowledge' of the great mystics: they were humanly aware of God,
of the things of God, even of the future, as a result of the
breaking through of God's presence from within, and not
through any experiential means of human knowing. Their
experience gives us the closest and strictest analogy, because
they became aware of God 'living' or being present within
their own souls, as ground of their own life and consciousness;
as we said above, they became aware of God more as subject
than as object.

And this leads us to what is theologically central. 'The
Spirit had not been given, because Jesus had not yet been
glorified ... "It is for your good that I am leaving you. If I
do not go, your Advocate will not come, whereas if I go, I will
send him to you." ' (Jn 7: 39 and 16: 7). Only when Jesus is
completely united with his Father (at the right hand of God)
is he able to send us his Spirit – ie his human awareness of
God that is now fully penetrated with the divine life. The
believing christian shares in the primordial revelation,
namely the consciousness of Christ, by Christ's gift of his
Spirit; by the Father sending his Spirit through the incarnate
and glorified Son. (The Word does not cease to be incarnate
in being glorified.) This is why the mystical experience is
both an analogy of the consciousness of Jesus and the fullest
development and exemplar of the christian faith: it is a
participation in the Spirit-filled consciousness of the Risen
Christ.

(b) *The process of revelation in the apostolic age*

The title of this section has been carefully chosen. It is not primarily the 'content' of revelation, or the 'object' of faith, that we are considering – both content and object are Christ himself – but the process of revelation: the process by which God's self-communication in the incarnation (revelation as an activity of God) is grasped or comprehended by men. We are looking at this process in the apostolic age, ie the whole period to which the New Testament bears witness. The word 'apostle' will be used in a loose sense for the eye-witnesses, if not of the public life of Jesus, at least of the resurrection (eg Paul), who first preached the good news. The apostolic age thus has a beginning. It has no determinate end, because it is not possible to say exactly what was 'the latest' stage of christian development attested in the corpus of writing that now forms our New Testament. Nor, it will be seen, is it meaningful to assign any end to the apostolic age, or to draw a chronological or theological line between the 'apostles' and the 'Church'.

In the case of Israel (the experience attested in the Old Testament) it is possible to consider the process of revelation in terms of 'event' and 'word'. The events, it has been suggested above, were simply the historical experience of Israel as seen by the secular historian. 'Word' in this pattern of thought is, first, the religious understanding of these events brought about in the consciousness of Israel by the action of God's Spirit (which of course is part of their historical experience); secondly, the notable verbal expression of this religious understanding, and in particular the sayings (oracles, hymns, etc) of the prophets that were specially treasured by Israel and preserved in her tradition as a force to guide present and future understanding.

The same thought-pattern can be applied, though less satisfactorily, to the time of Jesus and of the apostolic age. The events are Jesus himself, teaching and engaged in controversy, working miracles, dying, rising again, manifesting his risen and ascended life to the apostles, and finally sending his

Spirit. The coming of the Spirit at Pentecost is at once the end of the Jesus-time and the start of the apostolic age, though the two times are manifestly in continuity, and the 'apostles' (if we include Mary and Joseph) began to be eye-witnesses at the Annunciation. Similarly the coming of the Spirit is both event and word, and crosses our mental distinction between the two. The fourth gospel understands that Jesus sent the Spirit precisely to interpret the Jesus-time to the apostles, to enable them to understand truly or see spiritually what they had hitherto heard and seen mostly in a fleshy or this-worldly manner (Jn 14:26; 16:12-15).[2]

So the 'word' in this pattern of understanding is: first, the Word made flesh and the growth of Jesus' human consciousness; secondly, the outward manifestation by Jesus in word and deed of his own human grasp of God's design centred on himself; thirdly, the growing grasp in the minds of the disciples of the message in the messenger.[3] But christian faith in the full sense is not possible till Pentecost for two reasons: because the event as a whole has not occurred till Christ has risen; and because before the Spirit had not been given to the apostles to see the true meaning of all the Christ-events. So, finally, we have a fourth sense (or fourth and fifth senses) of 'word' in this context, namely the post-Pentecost mental grasp by the apostles of the full Christ-event, and its proclamation in words to the world. And, as has been said, this final apostolic prophetic word is a sharing in the Spirit-filled consciousness of Christ, which is 'word' in the first sense or first 'moment' of the process.

We must note that the proclamation by the apostles is not primarily of anything that Jesus said. The kerygmatic speeches in Acts, and Paul's brief reminder in 1 Cor 15:3-6, are a rough guide to the apostolic proclamation and (though they raise some other puzzles) show that the good news centred on Christ's death for our sins and rising for our justification (Rom 4:25). Paul's letters show very little awareness of anything Jesus said, or of his having told his converts about Jesus' teaching: but that he knew some of it is evident from 1 Cor 7:10 (the Lord's ruling about the permanence of marriage) and a few other passages. The collection and presentation of

Jesus' sayings is a logically and chonologically later process and belongs more to teaching (*didache* and *catechesis*) than to proclamation (*kerygma*), though no hard and fast line should be drawn between these activities or their content.[4] There is a strong tendency in the protestant tradition to search anxiously beneath the surface of our New Testament texts for the actual words of the mortal Jesus, as if these were in an exclusive sense 'the word of God'; as if without them we had nothing on which to base our faith. But, on the contrary, if all the words of Jesus had been lost, the basis of christian faith and the substance of the christian message would still remain in the bare outlines of the proclamation in a believing community.

We must next consider that the Spirit did not give to the apostles particular words, but eyes to see. As we thought when considering faith,[5] the most rudimentary recognition of the message in the messenger is already to some extent conceptualised and verbalised. So any words at any time used by the apostles to express their grasp of revelation are words 'inspired' by the Spirit. In what way any particular words they used may be called 'the word of God' will be considered in section (e) below. In general, however, we can at this point recognise that it is the apostles who, in their preaching and teaching, fulfil for the New Covenant the role performed by the prophets in Israel for the Old: it is their prophetic word, guided by the Spirit, that interprets the whole Christ-event to the world. Hence one finds that Paul heads his list of 'gifts' with those of 'apostles, prophets, teachers' (1 Cor 12:28): original proclaimers, interpreters, elaborators, one might say, though of course these roles could be fulfilled by the same person.

We may further reflect that 'the quest for the historical Jesus' can be seriously misconceived. Vastly interesting though it is, it is not in the strict sense essential for christian faith, which in any case has got along for quite a time without it. The mortal Jesus was not fully revelation: his life of deeds and teaching only constitute revelation in the light of his death and resurrection; their meaning was not, and could not have been, grasped by the disciples at the time they were witnessing them. Nor was it grasped then or later by many others; the events do not by themselves ground or produce faith. We have in fact only got the testimony of those who believed in the resurrection. Nor would any other testimony be the Gospel, capable of playing a part in constituting our faith. If a television audio-visual recording had been made of the life of Jesus, it would be a wonderful christian treasure, but it would be incomplete and inadequate, both on the part of Jesus who had not yet died or risen, and not yet reached the fullness of self-awareness; and on the part of the apostles, who did not yet believe. Hence the distinction between 'the Jesus of history' and 'the Christ of faith' is the wrong one. The necessary distinction is between the Jesus of history (the mortal Jesus) and the Risen Christ. And both are objects of faith. But the Jesus of history can only be truly grasped and understood (even, I would say, by himself) in the light of the Risen Christ.

The New Testament accounts as we have them are certainly laced throughout, and embroidered, by the apostles' subsequent faith-vision of the Risen Christ. (As has already been said, they would not be the Gospel if they were not.) But it is important to realise that they are not for that reason faulty testimony. On the contrary, they are all the more a witness to christian faith, ie to the revelational content or quality or meanings of the events to which they testify.

We have on our hands, in principle, the same problem about historical accuracy that arose over the Old Testament. Obviously, any factor of falsification or embroidery is more limited in the case of the New Testament by the much shorter time span, and by the fact that the Gospel was first preached in public before unbelieving and even hostile eye-witnesses. The element of embroidery can to some extent be traced in the growth of the gospel tradition(s) by modern scholarship: it must be understood as symbolic rather than literal, as testimony to the vivid faith-awareness or revelational meaning of events which might have been recorded (and possibly originally were) in more secular or literal fashion. Basic historical accuracy is, of course, essential. If Christ did not work any miracles of healing, for example, then there are no events of this kind in which revelational meaning can be discerned and expressed. But the evidence shows that he did: the miracles of healing belong to the earliest layer of gospel tradition; and why should the Pharisees need to interpret these actions as wrought by the power of Beelzebul, if there were none?[6] We are here up against the 'circularity' of a miracle. Whatever may be thought about any supposed miracles in the life of the Church, there is no theoretical difficulty about the God-man working miracles. But miracles are miracles only to the believer.[7] In stressing that the 'works' of Jesus are 'signs' and are the Father's testimony to the Son, which will only be recognised as such by him whom the Father draws to the Son, the fourth gospel is only developing a theology of miracles as 'powers' already present in Mark. In the synoptic tradition the miracles of Jesus are presented as signs that the power of God (kingship) is present in Jesus to conquer the power of the evil ones that subjugate God's people, and therefore as signs that the Day of the Lord (kingdom) is at hand. To the unbeliever the miracles are signs of diabolic work, or are just natural puzzles with no known natural explanation. A miracle *is* a secular event, even if to the believer it is not only a secular event; as a secular event, it must be thought to have some natural explanation, even if this is not yet known. One way of putting this is to say that divine causality is not in the same order of being as, and in competition with, natural causality, such that one is forced to regard a miracle as having a divine *or* a natural cause. Another way of putting it is to say that a miracle has both a material and a formal element: the material is a surprising and unexplained natural event; the formal is the religious sign-value. It is only the formal element that formally constitutes the event a miracle. Hence one cannot naturally or scientifically prove that any event is a miracle.[8] It is only a sign to one who can see what it is a sign of.

Centrally there is the event of the resurrection, of which all the other sign-events are themselves signs. But in what sense is Christ's rising from the dead a historical event? Only in a unique sense. He did not return to *this* life, like Lazarus, to live and die again; he was not resuscitated. He rose to eternal life. So, though the resurrection happened, it cannot be said simply to have happened in history. The life of the Risen Christ is not part of history; it is not in any temporal relation with this world's events, though of course awareness of it among others is. There is continuity between the historical Jesus and the Risen Christ, and it is this continuity which the apostles witnessed and attested: but it is a personal, not a temporal, continuity, and so not in any ordinary or manageable sense of the word a 'historical' continuity. Barth calls the resurrection an event outside history that limits history. Like a miracle, it has a material and historical 'under-side', but only its formal and non-historical reality makes it to be what it is. The resurrection of Christ is and can only be the object of faith: one cannot prove it, but only believe in it as a result of encountering the Risen Christ. (Once more, this is what the appearance to Thomas teaches.) The fact of the resurrection is outside the scope of the secular historian: as such, he cannot cope with it, any more than he can exclude it. It is an event at once 'earthly' and 'heavenly': the Ascension is a manifestation of its heavenly aspect. But, then, so is the life and death of the historical Jesus at once earthly and heavenly: for he is God living a human life, and dying a human death. The continuity of the earthly life and death with the Risen Christ is of the Person's humanity, and the Person is divine. Hence, as has been said, both the historical Jesus and the Risen Christ are the vehicle of revelation and the object of faith.

(c) *'According to the scriptures'*

It was noted above, in Chapter I (a), that Jesus presented himself to his disciples, not out of the blue, but in the whole historical context of the revelation to Israel, as its fulfilment. And so they came to understand him. It is integral to the apostolic preaching that they proclaimed Christ 'according to the scriptures', as a fulfilment of Israel's aspirations and of Old Testament prophecy. See especially Paul's 'recap' in 1 Cor 15: 3-4:

'First and foremost, I handed on to you the facts which had been imparted to me: that Christ died for our sins, in accordance with the scriptures; that he was buried; that he was raised to life on the third day, according to the scriptures; and that he appeared to Cephas etc ...'

Whatever one may think of the historical origins of the 'first sermons' given in Acts (2: 14-41; 3: 11-26; 4: 8-12; 5: 29-32; 10: 34-43; 13: 16-41), which preach Christ as a fulfilment of Old Testament passages, Paul writes a few years after his founding of the Church at Corinth early in 51 AD to say that he had then preached what he had previously received himself. So we seem to be safe in saying that, as soon as the apostles formulated their message at all, it was already in the form of preaching Christ according to the scriptures.

What scriptures? It was Professor C. H. Dodd who first went into this question in his truly fascinating and seminal book in 1952.[9] Though some aspects of Dodd's work have been modified by subsequent scholars, his main theses and principles about the use of the Old Testament in the New still stand, and are briefly as follows. From the outset the apostles appear to have had a basic list of Old Testament themes (themes rather than merely passages), and saw Christ as the coming-to-fullness of these themes (or aspirations of Israel). Certainly they had pet texts, and by exhaustive analysis of the Old Testament passages quoted in the New Testament Dodd is able to show the Bible-within-the-preaching, ie just what parts of the Old Testament the apostolic age used, and how it used them. But it is not just a matter of proof-texts. For instance: the gospel of Matthew quotes the Old Testament far more than the other gospels, and arranges much of its material to lead up to the punch-line: 'Thus was fulfilled what was said [by God] through the prophet Isaiah, when he wrote ...' The verb *plērōo* does not mean so much 'fulfil a prediction' as 'fill full' – bring to its fullness a theme of Israelite hope and Old Testament expression. This is why Matthew, who can quote the Old Testament accurately when he wants to, often produces an interpretative or paraphrased or conflated 'quotation': he is no fundamentalist; christian vision brings out the true meaning of the Old Testament sometimes only hinted at in the literal text. Adaptation of Old Testament texts in this way shows a prolongation of the general prophetic sense of the Old Testament, rather than a canonising of its exact verbal form. So this method is more than a set of proof-texts shared by the individuals and Churches who wrote the New Testament, and elaborated over the first two or three generations, though it is that. It is a vision of history. The faith and hope of Israel is fulfilled in Christ, so that Christ and his people are now the true Israel; not a 'new' People of God, but the one and only Israel brought to its consummation.

Dodd shows how the fundamentals of christian theology are all laid and contained here in this vision of the New Covenant as the filling-full of the Old: the doctrine of the Church as the true Israel; the foundations of christology; the doctrine of redemption (atonement). Christ is the true David, the true Moses, the true Isaac, the true Adam; he is the Rock from whence living waters flow; he is the true Pasch; his kingdom is the true Jerusalem, etc. Above all, in his death and resurrection is the true Exodus leading to the true and final covenant. The deuteronomist theology of the Old Testament saw God's dealings with Israel as a series of covenant arches, each fulfilment of promise leading, not to the end of the story, but to a new promise. So, in Christ, there is now the New Covenant foretold by Jeremiah. No Old Testament text is quoted more often in the New Testament than Jer 31: 31-34: 'The time is coming, says the Lord, when I will make a new covenant with Israel and Judah ... I will forgive their wrongdoing and will remember their sin no more.' And see Jer 32: 40: 'I will enter into an eternal covenant with them. ...'

The new and eternal, or final, covenant contains a final promise of revelation: even it is not the end of the story. The characteristic, if not only, use of the word 'reveal' or 'revelation' (*apokalypsis*) in the New Testament is, not for what God has revealed in Christ (this is more the *mysterion*, the long kept secret now let out), but for what is finally to be revealed in Christ's Coming: his victory is not a mere

matter of hope; it has already been won and secured for us
in the triumph of his resurrection from death and exaltation;
but its fullness has yet to encompass us and to be disclosed
to us. The book of 'Revelation' is about that End. So, too, for
instance, see 1 Peter 1.5ff:

'It is kept for you in heaven, and you, because you put
your faith in God, are under the protection of his power
until salvation comes – the salvation which is even now
in readiness and will be revealed at the end of time (v.5)
... when Jesus Christ is revealed (v.7) ... Fix your hopes
on the gift of grace which is to be yours when Jesus Christ
is revealed (v.13).'

Now all this adds up to a profound theological vision and
a very sophisticated theological method, which appears to
have been there in its main principles and content from the
beginning of the apostolic preaching. Where did the Galilean
fishermen get it from? It is hardly to be found in the teaching of the mortal Jesus preserved in the gospels, though there
are indications (eg Lk 24:44) that Jesus continually made
clear that the prophets would be fulfilled in him. Paul might
have been capable of it, but he says he received it. Luke is
quite explicit in saying that both the principles and the
content were taught to his disciples by the Risen Christ. He
makes the two disciples on the road to Emmaus the first
recipients of the vision and of the method:

' "How dull you are!" he answered. "How slow to believe
all that the prophets said! Was the Messiah not bound to
suffer this before entering upon his glory?" Then he began
with Moses and all the prophets, and explained to them the
passages which referred to himself in every part of the
scriptures.' (Lk 24: 25-27)

This set their hearts on fire (v.32). And that evening the
risen Lord appeared to 'the Eleven and the rest of the com-
pany' (v.34) and repeated the process with them. 'He opened
their minds to understand the scriptures' (v.45).

Theologically we may say that the apostles are given to share in the full consciousness of the Risen Christ.

(d) *Development within the New Testament*

If, as we have seen, revelation *is* Christ, within the whole historical setting of God's self-communication;

and if, revelation-received, or faith, is the total impact of Christ on human beings (such as the apostles) who recognise him as God's self-communication, in his historical setting, and 'according to the scriptures';

then: revelation is not basically words, not basically something stated. Nor can it adequately be put into words. It can only be experienced (first as self-awareness in Christ, then as personal relation in us), and witnessed to in a great variety of ways, ie it has to be lived.

As we saw when considering faith and doctrines, in Chapter 1 section (d), there is from the outset some conceptualisation in the grasp of Christ by, or encounter with Christ by, or impact of Christ on, the apostles. But the conceptual element is not itself, I would argue, part of revelation-as-given; nor is it all that we mean by revelation-as-received; it is not simply to be equated with faith; it is the doctrinal element in faith, which is controlled by the whole grasp of faith. Man does not first fully grasp reality, and then put his grasp into words or other actions. The expression in words, and in other ways, is itself a grasp and discovery of meaning. And yet the reality and our global grasp of it controls particular expressions.

There is very clearly a development of conceptualisation attested in the New Testament itself, ie in the doctrine of the earliest witnesses and teachers. This is so even, perhaps particularly, in such fundamental matters as the divinity of Christ and the meaning of his second Coming. Indeed, as we learn more about the layers of understanding present in our New Testament and about their temporal and local growth, we can see a variety of developments taking place in every christian doctrine. And it becomes a matter of fascination to try to discern how teachings were in some respects gradually corrected (just as in the constant re-editing process that lies behind the Old Testament), or how christian traditions of understanding in different places or Churches affected each other. For instance, the similarity of thought of Paul and John is most striking, but their theological vocabulary very different; and has Luke's infancy narrative been modified by or in a Johannine Church or milieu?

So there is no 'pure Gospel' in the sense of a more primitive and more genuine conceptual expression lying behind or at the basis of later or adapted understandings. The only basis is Christ himself. If a later understanding (in Matthew or Luke, say) modifies an earlier grasp (in Mark) of what Jesus said about the coming end and judgment, then we are right to conclude that 'later is better', if we have any sort of doctrine of inspiration – ie if we think the Spirit of truth is guiding the Church into all the truth (Jn 16: 13), and guiding the apostolic Church into this expression of it. Indeed, we must courageously assert that the truth (the understanding and its expression) that develops in the apostolic age is more God's message (*logos*) for us than what exactly the mortal Jesus said and what he meant by it at the time. The reason for this has been given earlier in this Chapter, in sections (a) and (b). If the later understandings of any point attested in the New Testament are simply different – well, they are different; if they conflict – well, they conflict. What criterion there might be for deciding in such cases for a 'better' or a 'worse' is a question we may leave for the moment.

It is interesting, though perhaps a digression in the present train of thought, to ask whether the faith of the apostles can be said to have grown or developed, and not simply their doctrine. I think it is accurate to say that the faith of the Church 'grew' or 'developed' or 'filled out'. It seems comparable to the process by which the consciousness of the mortal Jesus developed. Faith is man's grasp of God's self-communication in the Risen Christ. And man does not simply 'have' a grasp of reality and then merely set about 'expressing' it more and more adequately. All forms of expression are a deeper grasp of, a fuller discovery of meaning in, the reality that is globally comprehended at the outset.[10] But, of course, conceptual growth is not the only form of development of human expression, nor the primary one in this matter. The faith of the apostles grew by being lived and proclaimed. Then and now an individual Christian can more profoundly live, and therefore more profoundly express, his faith (in private and corporate prayer, self-sacrifice, mission, etc) without developing his conceptual expression beyond the global and rudimentary. And conversely.

Fr G O'Collins draws a distinction between the 'foundational' revelation given to (or faith of) the apostles and the 'dependent' revelation given to (or faith of) subsequent generations.[11] There is an obvious sense in which revelation to the apostles is foundational. They, the eye-witnesses, encountered Jesus uniquely (in a way other Jewish eye-witnesses did not) before his resurrection, and preserved a fuller and more perceptive memory of what he had said and done than others who only witnessed part and perhaps were not trying to learn. Whatever we may make of the details of the resurrection appearances, only the apostles were able to attest the continuity of mortal Jesus and risen Christ, and to learn to understand the former through the latter. Theirs in the Gift of Pentecost is the prophetic word that both witnesses to the events and their meaning, ie interprets them, and does so 'according to the scriptures'. It further makes sense, with O'Collins, to regard the Ascension, or closing of post-resurrection appearances, or final manifestation that Christ was now living an eternal and exalted life with God, as the closing of 'foundational revelation': because the apostles' encounter with Christ precisely as *unique* ended there; and because theirs is the foundation faith of the Church, which is preached and passed on down the ages. The idea of a 'deposit of faith' is not very helpful (and the expression is avoided in the *Constitution on Divine Revelation* of Vatican II), because, in view of the history of the word 'faith', it inevitably suggests a deposit of doctrines. There is no basic list of doctrines that has simply to be handed on. The deposit of faith is the experience of the apostles, which is attested in the New Testament. There is a foundation faith in or experience of Christ which can be said to have closed with the death of the 'last apostle', even though we know the word is vague in application.

But, at the same time, the distinction between foundational and dependent revelation is to some extent an arbitrary one, a purely schematic break in a continuous process, from the time of the apostles' meeting with Jesus, through Pentecost, to their death. Nor have we in the New Testament any testimony to the faith, and its expression, of the chosen eye-witnesses separable from the faith, and its expression, of the Church of the apostolic age: separable, that is, from the faith and thought-processes of a first generation of Christians who were not eye-witnesses, and of a second, and of a third.

In any case, there is no faith of the apostles that is prior to the faith of, the revelation experience of, the Church. For they are the Church, for instance at the Last Supper or at Pentecost. This is signified by their being Twelve. The distinction between foundational and dependent takes place within the faith of the Church, within the self-disclosure of God to man in Christ. The faith or doctrine of the Church does not follow logically or chronologically upon the faith or doctrine of the apostles. It is the living Church that is the 'locus' or 'place' of revelation, the People who believe in the risen Christ. Pentecost is the manifestation of what the Church is, the 'moment' of its self-understanding.

It was necessary for the apostles to see (materially) in order that they should believe (see spiritually). But they did not fully see spiritually till Pentecost, when they had ceased to be eye-witnesses. And it is this apostolic pentecostal faith that the Church lives, preaches and hands on. It is this faith on which the Christ of the gospel according to John pronounces his blessing.

Hence it might be better to drop the terminology of 'foundational' and 'dependent', and simply to say: for the faith of the Church it was necessary that, among the first group of believers in the risen Christ, there should be eye-witnesses to the historical Jesus.

(e) *What is the New Testament?*

The Church lived her faith for a long time – preaching it, thinking it, praying it, practising it – without a New Testament. Any idea of the need for one could have only grown gradually as the second Coming ceased to be thought of as imminent. A first canon had taken shape about 150 AD,[12] though the regarding of particular writings as 'scripture' is attested from about 120 AD. The writings that now form the New Testament are very varied. Many are letters, presumably written on one occasion and not retouched (though various readings for this or that verse could be circulating at an early stage). The letters are casual in various senses. Paul did not know he was writing scripture: he wrote a letter to a particular community for some immediate purposes. Some of his letters have got lost: First Corinthians refers to an earlier letter; Second Corinthians to a previous letter which is not First Corinthians. Some letters (Philemon and 3 John are extreme examples) have very little content and seem to have been accidentally preserved somewhere because of their authorship. The Revelation of John is in a very different key from the rest, and cannot have been the only early christian writing in the apocalyptic idiom: was it preserved because it was attributed to the apostle John? The gospels and Acts are very different: we know that they took their present shape in different Churches over two or three generations, and reflect the development of doctrine of the Churches; they only gradually came to be regarded as scripture, first in some places only, before being 'canonised' and receiving general recognition. To what extent were they canonised because their present form was, in later generations, wrongly attributed exclusively to eye-witness apostles?

At this distance we can see the process of canonisation of particular writings as 'scripture' to be the same as that at work in the formation of the Old Testament. By a gradual and continuous process of assessment the Church came to see that these writings reflected and expressed her faith, what she understood the apostolic faith to be.[13] Undue weight was no doubt put on supposed apostolic authorship. But the

'Gospel of Thomas' was not included; nor was 'The Teaching of the Twelve Apostles', though its date could be as early as 70 AD. The Epistle of Barnabas was excluded, the Epistle to the Hebrews included. Gabriel Moran writes: 'The Church could recognise these books as her own, even without external proofs, for the Scriptures were the objectification of the Church's self-understanding.'[14] Authoritative pronouncements as to the canon by Church Councils were in fact only subsequent ratifications of decisions made by christian communities about what genuinely expressed the Church's faith.[15]

So we may finally give an answer to the question that heads this section, as follows: The New Testament writings are that verbal witness to the faith of the apostolic Church, as it developed doctrinal expression, which gained eventual recognition as classic.

The 'inspiration' is primarily of the Church – of the Church both expressing her faith in writings (among other ways), and assessing these writings as the classic exposition of it. It was the Church, we believe, that was specially guided by God's Spirit in both these operations. The 'inerrancy' of the New Testament does not lie basically in the sphere of exactness in historical recording, or in explanatory statement, but in the fuller or more total sphere of faith, of human experience: the New Testament is a faithful witness to the original and enduring christian faith, ie to revelation, to man's grasp of God in Christ.

As we noted above in Chapter II, in section (a), Professor C. F. Evans has raised in a most cogent manner the question whether 'holy scripture' is really a christian idea at all, seeing that it originated in intertestamental Judaism; and whether it is really not a wrong or misleading idea after all. Is it a sound idea that this particular body of writings should be so rigidly set apart as the only inspired christian writings, subsequently normative for christian belief and thought? The idea runs into considerable difficulties.[16] The general christian sense of the Church may be trusted in its exclusion of some early works on the grounds of their general tone, but this does not justify a total severance in our thought, as if the 'best' elements in writings that eventually became non-canonical were in a different class from the weakest elements in the canonical writings. Neither Old nor New Testament can be cut off sharply from the literature contemporary with or immediately following their latest elements. 'The Old Testament in its later stages contains viewpoints which are characteristic of "post-biblical" Judaism, and similar elements in the New Testament have features of "post-apostolic" christianity.'[17] Nor can all the New Testament books be given equality of weight or importance, let alone all the New Testament sentences: they are not all equally 'holy scripture'.

As to the basic question about the whole idea of 'holy scripture', it is surely necessary to distinguish between the New Testament and the Old, if the idea is accepted that the religious vision and aspiration of Israel reaches its fullness in Christ, not by a continuous and unbroken process, but by the totally new and unprecedented fact (and 'intervention') of the incarnation. The mortal Jesus accepted the rabbinic idea of his time of the Old Testament as holy scripture, and taught it to his disciples – but with a marked difference from any idea of his time on two central points: he taught that the Old Testament was fulfilled in himself; and he taught his disciples to understand him in terms only of certain themes (and therefore passages) of the Old Testament and not of all of it; and also in terms of themes of rabbinic Judaism not prominent or scarcely found in the Old Testament. So he did not regard the Old Testament as 'holy scripture' in the ways the rabbis did. Nor did the apostolic Church. Hence, I suggest, it is a mistake for a Christian to regard it in the rabbinic way.

So too, there is a 'bible within the Bible' (though the phrase is misleading) for the Christian handling the New Testament, just as there was a selection made from the Old Testament by the apostolic Church. But I cannot see that this poses any theoretical problem, as long as one does not have a quasi-superstitious veneration for the actual wording, verse by verse, and set it in a class totally apart from any actual or possible alternative wording. God's Spirit, we have thought, guided the Church both in expressing itself in the New Testament writings and in selecting these writings as her 'canon' or rule. It is the Church so guided by the Spirit that selects within the New Testament: she has always found some books and some passages more expressive and nutritive of her faith than others. Some passages, and even books, she has hardly used. She has been right to see that the foundational elements in the New Testament are necessarily normative for future christian belief, simply because they are foundational in the sense examined. But she would now be mistaken, in the light of modern biblical scholarship, to imagine that the actual words of some books (eg Matthew, John, Peter in Mark) are the direct and first-hand teaching of eye-witness apostles; or to think that earlier is better, and that the words of apostles are 'more inspired' than those of others (what of Luke?). Paul is the outstanding teacher of the New Testament, and it seems that he was not an eye-witness to the life of Jesus. He says himself that he was chosen by God for the purpose. But it does not follow that everything he says is an exact witness to revelation.

And that leads us to a trickier question that was laid bare in the previous section. Is all the theology of the New Testament sound theology? It is easy enough to think of passages which the christian thinker has at least to gloss over: Paul's attitude to women in the Church; some of his directions about marriage given in view of an early expectation of the second Coming (about which he and other apostles were wrong). But there are deeper and more pervasive matters. It was a crucial problem to the early Christians that the Jewish leaders and people did not even now, after the resurrection and the preaching of the Gospel of the Risen Christ, accept him. (Christians long continued to think of themselves as within Judaism, as its true version, and we have often wrongly supposed a clear separation between Judaism and the Church, on either side, from Pentecost on.) We glanced earlier at Mark's attempt to grapple with this problem, viz God could not have meant the Jews to believe; so Jesus taught in parables to obscure his meaning, except to chosen disciples. Mark is certainly asking the right questions: but has he, or the christian school of thought he represents, given wrong answers? (The point is not whether the reader agrees with this particular understanding of Mark and of the 'messianic secret', but that in principle this sort of question can and must be put to the New Testament.) One cannot find a criterion within the New Testament itself for deciding what may be a sounder and what a less sound theology. Only the Church, constantly assessing her faith and its expression, could in principle decide such a matter. She decided a 'better' and a 'worse' among christian writings in choosing her 'rule'; she alone could choose within her rule, and come to hold that some apostolic expressions were more true, or more inspired, than others; and some mainly untrue, and so uninspired. Whether in practice she can do this is another matter, which must be looked at again.

It will be realised that, in the examination of Old and New Testaments in these pages, great stress has been laid on the People as the vehicle of inspiration and of God's guidance. ('I am with you always, to the end of time.') Protestant theology has in the main wished the New Testament, indeed the Bible, to have something like an independent existence of its own as the vehicle of God's self-communication to man. Man in this view meets God primarily in the Bible. (Hence the agonies of biblical criticism have been greater in the protestant than in the catholic tradition: in the former, the page itself, on or beneath the surface, must be made to yield the 'verbal words of God'.) Hence Old and New Testaments are regarded as on an equal footing. But this trend seems to disregard the incarnational quality of the kingdom of Christ. We have seen in examining faith, and will see further in the next chapter, that Christ lives, offers himself to man, and is to be encountered in an Israel, a People that he makes his own.

(f) *Is the New Testament the word of God?*

Some vagueness, if not confusion, prevails in our attitude to scripture owing to the various and loose uses of the phrase 'word of God', and this section will attempt to clarify the situation. In Roman Catholic liturgy the Reader announces after the first reading at Mass, 'This is the word of the Lord', to which all reply, 'Thanks be to God'. Do we know quite what we mean? Do we mean the same for an Old Testament and a New Testament reading? For the moment we shall concentrate on the New Testament, leaving further consideration of the Old Testament to the last chapter.

Confusion over 'word' goes with confusion over 'truth'. To the hebraic mind truth is opposed not to error, as is mainly the case in western thought, but to lying and deceit. Christ is the Truth, first because he is the veracious and reliable witness to, and self-disclosure of, God; secondly, because he is the authentic Son of David, Shepherd, Vine, etc.

In western or hellenic speculative thinking there tends to be a misleading interchange between truth and reality. This can only be avoided if we retain the word 'truth' for man's conceptual grasp and verbal expression of reality. There can be a mental truth, a meaning or content grasped, and a verbal expression of that content. The two are not separable because, as has been observed above, we grasp meaning in the act of expressing it, even when the expression does not exhaust the meaning or content. But both are a human grasp of reality (abstract content and concrete verbal expression), and distinct from the reality grasped. Hence, within this hellenic thought-pattern, the consciousness of Christ is basically the Truth with a capital T. His verbal expression is concretely truth. As far as we, the believers, are concerned: Christ is the reality grasped; the 'inspired' (in the sense examined) verbal expression of the eye-witnesses is concretely the truth.

In the *Logos* doctrine of John's gospel there are two components. The more prominent is the hebraic and biblical notion of God's creative word, his utterance that makes things happen ('he spoke and it was done'). There is also present the hellenic idea of self-expression. In the present discussion we may concentrate on this latter component, because it has been in western thought and over this component that the ambiguities have occurred. So, in these hellenistic terms, we need to distinguish:

(a) Christ is the 'Word of God'. In the life of God himself
the Second Person is (in this thought pattern) the expression
of God the Father to himself. In the incarnation God expresses
himself wholly to man in human terms and in human history
– 'Philip, anyone who has seen me has seen the Father' (Jn
14: 9) – for man could only grasp God when put into such
terms. Only the Word incarnate merits a capital 'W': whatever the relation between God and scripture is thought to be,
the latter is not hypostatically united to the Word of God.

(b) The expression 'word of God' is used for the abstract
truth, meaning, or content, that is grasped in Christ by christian faith, independently of any words that we may use to
express that meaning. This abstract sense of 'word of God' is
the same as that of 'the Gospel', when we use that phrase for
the essential christian message, abstracting from any particular gospel or any other formulation; though it cannot
exist in our minds as an abstract content independently of
some formulation.

In a whole host of New Testament passages, in the phrase
traditionally translated in English 'the word of God', the
Greek word *logos* means 'message'. And the translation of
logos by 'word' (which does not mean 'message'), and the
equivalent in other modern languages, has greatly contributed
to the rigid veneration for the actual words in which the
message is expressed. Luke uses the phrase in the explanation
of the Parable of the Sower, 'The seed is the message of God'
(Lk 8: 11), but Mark and Matthew do not, so presumably it
does not go back to Jesus. But of course the word *logos* is
often used in the gospels for Jesus' message, and in the fourth
gospel there is repeated insistence that the message or words
of Jesus are not his own but 'the word of God' (Jn 3: 34; cf
12: 49; 17: 14). Luke in Acts, and Paul, often refer to the
christian message, the Gospel, as the *logos* or message of God
(Acts 4: 31), or 'message of the Lord' (Acts 6: 7; 13: 49);
again, 'the sword of the Spirit, which is the message of God'
(Eph 6: 15). And Paul insists that God's message is not the
message of men, but truly the message of God (1 Thess 2: 13).
Behind this lies the Old Testament usage of 'word of God'
for the message of the prophets. But we can see that what is

in mind is chiefly the abstract sense, the Gospel message, rather than any particular words in which it is couched and conveyed.

(c) So, finally, we come to the actual wording of the New Testament, the verbal expression of God's message in various ways. The question before us is whether this can appropriately be called 'the word of God'.

The New Testament is the only remaining verbal witness to the apostolic experience and teaching. And it is an expression guided by the Spirit. So it can certainly be said to contain a divine and not a human message. But it is misleading to call it 'the word of God', because the phrase inevitably suggests some idea of divine dictation of these particular words, an equal value of all verses or sentences, a timelessness and freedom from cultural conditioning which no human words can have, and a direct communication by God to me through the book which by-passes the living Christ living in his people. To call the New Testament the word, and not just the message, of God inevitably suggests that God is talking to me direct through these particular words. This is a myth. Like all good myths it enshrines and expresses a deep religious truth. But, as with all myths, it can produce disastrous distortions if taken literally.

The words of the New Testament are words of man about the Word of God, even though they are human words that result from the assistance of God's Spirit (in a fuller and more definitive way than words arising from non-christian religious experience[18]). They cannot have the ultimacy that 'words of God' would have. These words of man sometimes quote the words of Jesus: these have a further ultimacy (when we are sure we have them), and it seems that collected sayings of Jesus were the first writings to be treated by Christians as scripture on a level with the Old Testament; but even so the development and historical conditioning of the human consciousness of Jesus must not be overlooked.

The principal witness to the apostolic experience remains, of course, the Church herself. So the New Testament can only be the (verbal) word of God within the Church. The whole life of the Church in its varied forms of expression is in a fuller sense God's word or expression, only we do not use the phrase for this wider self-expression of Christ in his Body.

NOTES

1. See Gabriel Moran, *Theology of Revelation*, New York, Herder, 1966, especially pp 63-76.
2. Many commentators consider that John 14 and 15-16 are two versions, a shorter and a longer, of the same discourse material.
3. See above, p 2.
4. See James Barr, *The Bible in the Modern World*, London, SCM, 1973, p 139.
5. Above, p 9.
6. The apologetic and counter-apologetic about the powers of the Spirit or of evil spirits *could* only belong to the *Sitz im Leben Jesu*.
7. See John Marsh's Introduction to the Pelican edition of *St John*, Penguin Books, 1968, p 65.
8. See Francois Rodé, *Le miracle dans la controverse moderniste*, Paris, Beauchesne, 1965; Louis Monden, *Signs and Wonders*, New York, Desclée, 1966; Hugo Meynell, *God and the World*, London, SPCK, 1971, chapter 4.
9. C. H. Dodd, *According to the Scriptures*, London, James Nisbet, 1952; Fontana Books, 1965.
10. For Newman's understanding of the development of doctrine in these terms, and for the similar but more philosophically developed analysis of Maurice Blondel, see Jan Walgrave, *Unfolding Revelation*, London, Hutchinson, 1972, pp 293-321.
11. *Theology and Revelation*, Cork, The Mercier Press, 1968, pp 49-50. The distinction between original and dependent revelation was made by Tillich.
12. An agreement on what is accepted today as the canon of the New Testament was reached at the end of the fourth century, after a long and complicated process. 'But it took centuries after that before it prevailed everywhere': Kurt Aland, *The Problem of the New Testament Canon*, London, Mowbray, 1962, pp 8-14. 2 Peter, 2 and 3 John, James, Jude, Hebrews and Revelation were the last to gain universal acceptance in east and west. Meanwhile, up to the fourth century agreement, a number of writings not eventually included in the canon continued to hold canonical status in some Churches.
13. See Aland, op. cit., p 13.
14. *Theology of Revelation*, p 108.
15. Aland, op. cit., p 18.
16. The problem has been further considered by James Barr, *The Bible in the Modern World*, London, SCM, 1973. Barr handles the questions that arise with great clarity and dexterity, and I have learned much from his treatment. But in my view he does not quite reach a solution, as he concentrates too exclusively on the Book, and too little on the People.
17. Barr, op. cit., p 117.
18. See Chapter 2, section (c), above.

Chapter Four

THE FAITH OF THE CHURCH

(a) *Social dimensions of faith*

As has been seen, there is no clear demarcation between the foundational faith of the apostles and the dependent faith of post-apostolic Christians. Nor can any distinction be made between the faith of the apostles and the faith of the Church, for the privileged eye-witnesses are also the Church.

From the nature of the case the New Testament is evidence of a first generation in which the Church grew by the preaching of the Gospel to non-christian adults. Hence, 'faith is from hearing' (Rom 10: 17). Paul concludes this summary of his argument by the rather vague phrase, 'and hearing is through Christ's message'.[1] This could mean either 'message about Christ' or 'message from Christ'. Hence, too, in this situation faith is often seen in terms of an adult response to a preached Gospel. However, nowhere in the New Testament is there any suggestion of a direct individual-to-God faith that by-passes the christian community.[2]

After this first stage, however, the christian community grows, and eventually grows principally, by self-propagation, ie by the christian family.[3] (This is the basic reason why catholic theology wishes to call christian marriage a sacrament.) In either case the believing community comes first: one either joins it from outside or is born within it. For the 'born Christian' personal faith grows within the community as a share in its faith. This corresponds to the way human beings develop in the natural sphere: we do not arrive in the world as fully constituted persons, but progressively become, or strive to become, persons by ever deepening and ever widening relationships to other persons; society forms persons, and adult persons continually refashion society.

The facts need to be borne in mind by those Christians who say they have no use for organised religion or for the institutional Church. Christianity is a people, a community. Any form of human society, starting with the family, has *some* form of outer structure or 'institution'. One may (rightly or wrongly) complain that the existing forms of christian structure have become irrelevant, out of date, distorted, etc, and seek to change them. But Christians cannot be thought of as a series of granulated individuals who do not form a body, a community, the household of God.

Karl Barth has stressed that faith comes about by Christ laying hold of man, not man laying hold of Christ. It is in and through the existing christian community that Christ presents himself to, and addresses, us, whether we are born inside or outside the believing community.

The Church is always more than the people and their outer framework or institutions in their visible and historical aspects. It is, in the strictly theological sense of the term, a mystery. Indeed, it is *the* mystery, the presence and action of the risen and triumphant Christ made visible in human society. When we say 'the Church' we of course mean the whole people and not only its institutional elements. But in theological reflection we must also mean 'the Spirit in the people'. And in that ultimate sense the faith of the Church is always more than the here and now actual faith of its members. It is the witness of the Spirit, and so in principle a whole and perfect faith. Hence the faith of the Church, the Word incarnate in the Church, challenges the Church's patterns of thought, of behaviour, of structure. A merely human message or doctrine could be fully 'possessed' and simply passed on in tranquillity; but the Gospel continually lays an urgency and an imperative on man which he never adequately satisfies or fulfils.

Hence in theological tradition the 'sense of the praying and believing Church' (*sensus orantis et credentis ecclesiae*) has always been seen as a guide to the authentic belief of Christians. The phrase is meant to indicate the whole christian experience, christian life, not merely the articulated thoughts of Christians, which can themselves never be more than a formulation of faith-experience. (Hence theological language can only have meaning for believers, for those who share the experience it articulates.) Those with a responsibility for teaching in the Church are within, not above, the *sensus fidelium*: their task can only be to formulate what is already the faith of the Church, which they themselves received from the Church; not to tell a hitherto ignorant Church what its faith is. We shall see later how full use is made by the Orthodox Churches of this concept of the 'consensus' or 'sense' of the Church.

(b) *'Loss' of faith*

In these days the process in the 'born Christian' of personalising a faith that has been drawn from and nourished by the faith of the family and of the wider community is often, if not always, a series of challenges. It could well be so even in a christian society, in so far as growing understanding in secular fields continually presents intellectual challenges, and demands that the doctrinal or intellectual formulation of our faith should be at least as advanced as our development in other fields, and should be related to this other development. Many come to feel alienated from their childhood faith, if they retain only a childhood notion of it when they have become more adult in other spheres. But an additional challenge is made by a pluralist and mainly secularised society, which has no use for christian or any religious belief. The home and school society will have supported and nourished faith; the wider society explicitly or implicitly denies its relevance to adult life. A young person may come to feel he has been alienated by family and perhaps school from the contemporaries with whom he wishes to belong. Very many experience the need to wander for a time, or to contract out of a committed christian life in order to stand over against it and come to a personal option for or against. If the option is in some cases against, this should not cause surprise: there is always a mystery at the heart of faith, the mystery why some believe and others do not, because it is ultimately God's self-gift and not man's acquisition as a result of any human process. Further, in a supposedly christian society many may rub along without either any real personal engagement or any need to opt decisively out. But in our pluralist society it is increasingly impossible to be a believing Christian without a fairly strong measure of personal commitment. At one time 'believers' and 'unbelievers' were charted on a map. Today the real line is between the committed and the uncommitted. And the committed know very well that the line passes right through themselves: we are never wholly committed; we never have a perfect faith; the sense of reality in our faith tends to ebb and flow. Most believers know from their own experience what it is not to believe.

How central in true commitment is assent to the Church's doctrines? It may help here to use Newman's distinction between real and notional assent. These are not necessarily alternatives: I can have a notional assent or I can also have a real assent. A notional assent to the authoritative teaching of the Church is a mere non-denial of some statement which in fact hardly corresponds to or influences any concern in my life. Real assent to what the Church teaches amounts to saying: 'I don't simply accept this as what "they" teach; it expresses just what I believe and try to live by.' It is not an assent to a statement presented from outside, but an assent to a formulation of experience given from within the experience. Conversely, it is possible to have a real assent but notional dissent. Dissent from an official doctrine is not necessarily alienation from the Church's experience (though it can be): it may be dissatisfaction with a particular way of formulating the Church's experience which in fact I share; or failure to understand that way of formulating it; it may be simply part of the process of intellectual challenge, which is intrinsic to the passage from a more elementary to a more developed intellectual grasp. The Church's 'doctrines' do not exist in isolation from each other as items in a package. They are interlocked, and the human mind needs to hold convictions together in an interrelated system: developments in one area of thought throw other areas out of line or out of perspective; answering a question at one level raises questions at deeper levels. Indeed, the intellectual or theological process is without end, but its task remains that of striving to explore and formulate more and more adequately the lived and contemporary christian experience, not of simply propelling itself in a detached and merely cerebal way.

A sense of 'loss of faith', or loss of the sense of reality in faith thus belongs to normal christian development. It is also characteristic of more profound and mature christian development, as is universally attested by mystical writers. The 'dark night of the soul' is a stage in spiritual progress in which the whole intellectual or conceptual side of faith goes dead and meaningless; no form of human expression – conceptual, poetic, pictorial, or any other – any longer has meaning; the spirit of man is summoned by God to hold on to him in a 'blind' and unconsoling faith, in order that the affective powers of man may go out to find and savour God beyond the point where intellectual effort can reach. This brings out what is true of all faith, that it is not basically a conceptual grasp, but a deep and total personal response.

We reflected to some extent in Chapter II, section (c), that God reveals himself in all human experience; and in Chapter I, section (c), on the continuity between christian faith and human experience. Man experiences himself as searching, as constantly transcending himself and reaching beyond his present, or indeed any imaginable, attainments. He is driven to seek more knowledge, more justice, more freedom. In his aesthetic activities he glimpses, touches upon, an absolute that he can never realise. Above all he does so in the central human experience of love. In the very heights of his experience (as well as in its depths) he grasps for, and so is dimly aware of, a wholeness, a permanence, a perfection of consummation. None of this is 'proof' that such an absolute, that God, exists. And one must respect the intellectually sincere and often heroic position of many an agnostic who would really like God to exist, but cannot honestly be convinced that he does. But without such a human experience of groping, man would not be able to recognise God when he did communicate himself;[4] without it, the language of religious belief could not convey any meaning whatever to an agnostic. So christian revelation is interpreting common human experience. It is proclaiming fully what God has done for all, whether they recognise it or not. It is saying that man in fact searches for the absolute in life, experiences a continual self-transcendence, only because he is made for the Kingdom of Christ; that he would not be man, would not have the characteristically spiritual dimension of human experience, if God had not made him for himself.

Hence we are never able to say that a man has 'no faith' or has 'lost his faith'. The modern western agnostic is the product of centuries of christian thought-patterns, his whole culture is laced with and conditioned by them, even if he disavows their source. And if we are to interpret the sincere gropings of the agnostic as an unarticulated faith, how much more must we think this of the perhaps temporarily disoriented Christian?

NOTES

1. The Greek noun in this case is *rēma*.

2. *pisteuein eis* seems to be a christian coinage for being or becoming a Christian.

3. 1 Cor 7:14, according to its most obvious interpretation, is already evidence of the idea that children of christian parents (of even one christian parent) are already 'holy' simply from their parentage and without mention of baptism.

4. Bultmann speaks of man's pre-grasp or pre-understanding of God (*Vorverständnis*). Barth had asserted man's inability to contribute anything to faith, as faith was totally God's gift. Brunner objected that man must at least be able to receive God's gift, to grasp God presenting himself. Barth's position arises from his considering man without christian faith as 'purely natural' man. But the fact that man gropes for and reaches out towards God is already the work of Christ's Spirit.

Chapter Five

SCRIPTURE AND TRADITION

Reflection on the process of revelation and its relation to scripture has already shown us that from the beginning of Christianity the living Church is the 'locus' of revelation and of its expression. Only the living Church can sift authentic from inauthentic expression. This leaves us with two questions, vital for our method as christian thinkers today. The first question, classically known as the problem of scripture and tradition, can be formulated thus: what is the theological criterion of christian truth for the christian thinker today? The second question is whether there are authoritative organs in the Church for settling controversy about christian truth: ie organs which can use the theological criterion authoritatively. I propose to tackle these two questions in this and the next chapter, aware of their complexity, and so without any pretension of giving them exhaustive treatment; but attempting at least to establish what I understand as the correct framework in which they should be discussed.

(a) *Luther and Trent*

What Luther challenged and attacked was, not some theory of the transmission of doctrine, but traditional practices such as indulgences, private and chantry Masses, the celebration of Mass without the people receiving Communion, Communion under one kind, concentration on the elevation and adoration of the Sacrament – not to mention parasitic monasteries, the worldliness of clerics, the abuse of power. He appealed, as one might say Francis had done three centuries before, in a different kind of protest, to the spirit of the Gospel. In controversy he was inevitably led to challenge the doctrines implied by and underlying the practices in question. This is a fair and important challenge: faith is not expressed solely in more official doctrines, but also and more profoundly in the way Christians live. So the doctrinal challenge raised the question of the official Church's authority. What was the value of the practices that had become accepted and in that sense traditional or of ways of thinking that the Church had developed in the course of her long life? All at the time (and for long afterwards) shared a simple view of the New Testament as a set of early contemporaneous writings of apostolic authorship: so it was possible to question the value of ideas and practices that had developed 'since scripture'. *Sola scriptura* became the battle cry. Nothing, however good, could be compulsory, if not directly attested in scripture. But there could be bad developments as well as good, and the only criterion or deciding authority was the text of the New Testament.

Trent replied to the challenge precisely in the terms in which it was put. Not only scripture, but the traditional practices of the Church are a guide to what Christ wills for his Church. Furthermore, the (official) Church has the authority to interpret scripture.

It is of great importance for the history of the question to appreciate that Trent and Luther were using the word 'traditions' in the same sense of customary practices.[1] What Trent said has so often been mistranslated. It opens its 'Decree on accepting scripture and traditions (*sic*)' by speaking of the Gospel which Jesus first promulgated by his own mouth and then instructed his apostles to preach, 'for it (the Gospel) is as it were the source of all saving truth and of all regulation (or ordering) of custom'.[2] So far, surely, complete agreement with Luther.

The text continues as follows: 'This truth and ordering of observance is contained in written books and in unwritten traditions, which (traditions) were received by the apostles either from the mouth of Christ himself or at the dictation of the Holy Spirit, and have come down to us as though passed from hand to hand.'[3] The Council speeches show various things about this statement: in speaking of *traditiones* the Fathers were uniformly concerned with traditional practices, some of which are attested in scripture and some not (so scripture and traditions are not necessarily alternatives in their thought); they were fully aware that some observances or forms of Church life (such as Lent, religious orders) did not go back to apostolic times, but they restricted their official statement to those that did, contenting themselves with saying that the saving truth of the Gospel is contained not only in the written books but also in apostolic traditions of observance, not attested in scripture, but handed on in a practical manner ('from hand to hand').[4] Thus Trent says far less in this statement than has often been supposed.

The Council completes its statement in the same (very long and complicated) sentence by saying that: 'it accepts and venerates with the same piety and reverence all the books of both Old and New Testaments – for God is the only author of both – as well as these same traditions, concerning both faith and observance (*mores*), as received either from Christ's lips or from dictation of the Holy Spirit, and preserved by continual succession in the Catholic Church.' In view of the various things Trent is often taken to have said, the following comments on this passage seem necessary.

(i) Trent made no pronouncement at all about doctrinal formulations or about practices that had developed after apostolic times, though it discussed some of the problems connected with these.

(ii) Hence Trent does not say that it regards such post-apostolic traditions with the same reverence as scripture. It only says that it receives observances originated by the apostles with the same reverence as scripture, without stating which these observances are (the shape of the eucharistic liturgy was instanced in discussion).

(iii) The Council's decrees were not concerned with the later discussion about Tradition as a continuing source of authoritative teaching in the Church.

(iv) The discussion show that the Council Fathers realised

that not all apostolic traditions, even those attested in scripture, had necessarily to be observed (eg that a bishop should
be a man of only one wife), and drew a distinction between
practices concerning or implying truths of faith, and merely
disciplinary or ceremonial observances, which they termed
traditiones de moribus. Hence, when distinguished from
fides, mores at Trent means customary observances and does
not mean 'morals'. So Trent does not make any explicit pronouncement on moral teaching: the argument was not about
moral teaching. Still less does it speak of tradition in the
post-apostolic Church as a continuing source of authoritative
teaching about morals.

(v) The term 'faith' is used in a far wider sense at both
Florence and Trent that merely to designate 'doctrines'[5]:
similarly today we speak of 'practising the faith', giving a
broad and untechnical sense to the word. At Trent, then, it
is the word *fides* not the word *mores* which covers christian
conduct and morals.[6]

(b) *The two-source theory*

It has often been pointed out that Trent avoided saying that
'saving truth' was contained partly in scripture and partly in
tradition,[7] thus leaving open the opinion that all truths
necessary for salvation are attested in scripture. But Trent
also accepted the idea, and post tridentine theology assumed
it, that Christ must have explicitly told the apostles, or the
Spirit made clear to them, doctrines of catholic faith not
attested in scripture (such as the seven sacraments, purga-
tory), and that these were passed on orally by them and found
expression in later christian literature. So basically it can
be said that Trent canonised *a* two-source theory of revelation, oral and written, understanding 'revelation' as 'doctrinal
propositions', or more simply doctrines; but doctrines that
were. there from the beginning as part of the deposit of
doctrine. It did not canonise or give grounds for any other
two-source theory.

We have seen many reasons for not understanding the

process of revelation by such categories of thought, and will not rehearse them here. But this simple and propositional picture of two streams of doctrinal teaching issuing from the apostles has not got quite the historical improbability that has sometimes been attributed to it. Trent and Luther were, after all, basically talking about christian practices. Prayer for the dead, for instance, with its possible implications of the dead being in a state between earth and heaven, is attested extremely early. It was not stretching imagination very much to think that 'before the death of the last apostle' this practice was sanctioned in christian Churches. (Indeed, for all we know it was.) Part of the importance attributed in post-tridentine theology to the writings of the Fathers of the Church was that, in reflecting on contemporary christian life, they gave written witness at a more or less early date to the unwritten traditions supposedly handed down from the apostles. There is no suggestion in this tridentine two-source theory that apostolic traditions had remained purely oral right down to the time of Trent. However, the theory runs into increasing implausibility the later is the doctrine – or the explicitation of doctrine – that it is invoked to account for.

There is, of course, a greater reason for giving a place of special honour to the Fathers: simply that they are christian classics. Like all classics, they are made or recognised as such by the community whose values they reflect and notably express. The faith of the Church saw in them its own features mirrored in a more perfect way than in lesser and untreasured writings. (The process which canonised Old and New Testaments continues: it is a process in a living, believing community.) And, like all classics, they thereafter exert a strong formative force on the life of the community.

The writings of the Fathers, however, are themselves very largely commentaries on scripture. From this two things follow. First, they set up a tradition, or traditions, of interpreting scripture. Trent was aware of this factor, and so went on to say[8]: 'The Council decrees, in order to restrain irresponsible minds, that no one shall presume, in matters of faith and of observances that have a bearing on christian doctrine,[9] so to rely on his own conceptions as to twist scrip-

ture to his own meaning in a way contrary to the meaning
that holy mother Church has held and holds – for it is for
her to decide the true meaning and interpretation of scripture
– nor have the audacity to interpret scripture in a way contrary to the unanimous consensus of the Fathers.'

The second thing that follows from the fact that the works
of the Fathers are largely commentaries on scripture, is that
they cannot be thought of as a source of, or witness to, accepted
christian doctrine that is separable from scripture. Rather
are they a witness to the accepted interpretation of scripture.

It would not be possible or profitable here to examine all
the attempts of post-tridentine theology to explain the process
of handing down revelation in the Church.[10] They were
based on a propositional view of what was being handed on,
and broadly speaking they held to two sources (*fontes*) of
revelation, scripture and tradition. The latter term, now in
the singular, had ceased to mean 'customary practices of
ancient origin' and came to refer mainly to established
doctrine. It came to include not only doctrines not attested
in the New Testament yet supposedly given to the Church
by the apostles, but also doctrinal systems that had later
become established in the course of the Church's history.
However, in the decades before the Second Vatican Council
theologians had become uncomfortable about the text-book
phrase 'two sources', wishing to maintain both the primacy
of scripture and the dependence of all subsequent christian
thinking on scripture. Hence 'scripture in the light of tradition' became the characteristic way of stating the Church's
criterion for discerning doctrinal truth and error.

The *schema* on the subject prepared for discussion by
Vatican II bore the title *De Fontibus Revelationis* ('Concerning the Sources of Revelation'). This occasioned the Council's
first major disagreement: both the title, with its suggestion
of two sources, and the whole treatment, were felt to go back
to abandoned patterns of thought. The document was sent
back for complete revision before discussion could begin.
The *Dogmatic Constitution* eventually approved and promulgated by the Council bears the title, *De Divina Revelatione*

('Concerning Divine Revelation'), and opens up a new approach to the concepts of revelation and tradition.

(c) *What is tradition?*

Patient perusal of the various theories of 'tradition' leaves one with the conviction that catholic theology of the period was all the time dealing with derivative manifestations, and had not succeeded in coming to grips with not so much a basic concept as the basic reality, the basic process, from which secondary factors flow.

What in fact is handed on by the Church?

The radical answer to this question – which is then seen also to answer the question, *How* is it handed on? – may seem at first sight very inward-looking. The radical answer can only be, *the Church*. The living Church hands on, perpetuates in history, the living Church. The Church, one might say, is history: it is living and believing men and women, perpetuating their faith in succeeding generations, and expressing it in manifold ways.[11]

But, when one says 'the Church hands on the Church', as a theologian one is not using the expression 'the Church' (either as subject or object of the sentence) simply for the visible human reality as historically discernible. Theologically, the Church is Christ's people indwelt and animated by his Spirit. Hence the radical theological answer to the question we have set out with is: Christ hands himself on in his People. The Body of Christ perpetuates the Body of Christ. If ultimately Christ *is* revelation, then it is Christ who is handed on, perpetuated, in a living People. Or, as we saw above,[12] the consciousness of Christ is imparted to the believing community by the gift of his Spirit to them.

Hence the Church is herself revelatory. She is so in her whole way of living (worshipping, thinking, teaching, preaching, caring, etc) in response to the Gospel. In this sense revelation (dependent revelation) continues: it does not close with the Ascension of Christ or the end of the apostolic age.

It is important to insist at this point that we are not dealing simply with large, reassuring, theological concepts, but
with real live people. To say that the Church hands on the
Church is to emphasise the incarnational nature of God's
saving action. God dwells in us by his Spirit, making us
Christ's Body. 'Revelation can be shown forth adequately
only in people', writes Gabriel Moran.[13] This can be understood of the saints: in various ways they exhibit and manifest
what christian life really is. It can more basically be understood of christian parents – though the two categories are not
necessarily distinct! After the first age of preaching the
Gospel to non-christians, the chief way in which the Church
hands itself on is by christian marriage. Christian parenthood
brings succeeding generations of children to Christ, it unites
the Church to the Bridegroom throughout history. (We need
to recall at this point what was said above about the faith of
the Church.) Revelation is of God's love, and love can only
be found in people, given to people.

Consequently it is not possible to give an adequate explanation of the relationship between scripture and tradition
without introducing a third term, the living Church. The
living Church hands on the living Church: the sentence states
all at once what is handed on, by whom, and how. The
Church, we must recall, did not begin after the apostolic age:
its birth as a believing community is signalised by Pentecost.
It preached its message about the mortal Jesus and the living
Christ from then on, It uninterruptedly developed its expression and understanding of that message, both verbally and in
a host of other ways. The New Testament is, as we defined it
above,[14] that verbal witness to the faith of the apostolic
Church, as it developed doctrinal expression, which gained
eventual recognition as classic. As these writings came by
degrees to reach a definitive form, to circulate, to be more and
more widely accepted, they became the classic expression of
the Gospel, the apostolic faith. So they became normative:
because revelation took place in history, and these writings
contain the only evidence of what happened and how it was
understood; and because a culture with only one classic must
be guided and directed by it thereafter. Yet it is only in a

living and believing Church that the New Testament can be normative, because there is constant interaction between the Church and the Book: the Church (real people) meditates on it, prays from it, preaches it, examines its meanings endlessly, and so nourishes and forms her own life from it; but she also balances, assesses and selects,[15] shifting emphases and preoccupations in different ages, as she is stimulated by the thought, scholarship and cultural problems of the age she lives in.

Professor Cullmann has argued that, after the canonisation of the New Testament, the Church no longer has a role as a norm.[16] He grants that it was the living Church that progressively expressed itself in the New Testament, and eventually by internal discernment segregated canonical from apocryphal writings, and finally fixed the canon of the New Testament as a norm. But he argues that thereby the Church asserted that she was not a norm to herself; hence, that tradition has an essential role to play up to the 'definition' of the canon, but not thereafter *as a norm*. In this argument, however, Cullmann appears to be understanding tradition in a too superficial and secondary sense of the outward traces in history of the mystery-life that is handed on. But the life of Christ continues to be handed on: it is not only scripture that is handed on. The Church moves forward into ever new experiences, new cultures, new challenges, and understands the Gospel ever afresh. So, granted that the New Testament remains normative for her understanding of the Gospel, does the Church's response to new experiences mean nothing and add nothing? Was nothing of lasting value achieved in the interaction with the hellenism of the first few centuries? Was anything lost? Was nothing acquired definitely at Nicea, at Ephesus, at Chalcedon? Surely only the Church can answer these questions – or continue in succeeding generations to put them, and to try to answer them.

Hence the answer to Cullmann would appear to be as follows. By fixing the canon of the New Testament the Church asserted that she was not a self-sufficent norm. But the very act of canonising shows that she is *a* norm; and she must continue to be a norm of understanding the Gospel, the message of God, in the developing and variously new worlds she enters.

(d) *Is Luther answered?*

The question that emerged from Martin Luther's protest is: What, for the Church then and for the Church today, is the criterion of christian truth? Has the question ever had a satisfactory answer?

The classical protestant answer, *sola scriptura*, was not for Luther so much a worked-out theory as a slogan of protest and a method. For protestantism it is a way of life which must be judged by its fruits. It is first and foremost a spirituality. It nourishes Christians from the Bible. It constantly renews Christianity as a religious vision and a religious challenge, and prevents it from degenerating into a system or a compromise. But where in all the Bible, or in all the New Testament, is one to put the emphasis? On the justification of the sinner by the wholly gratuitous mercy of God? That emphasis is obviously a historical accident and not a self-authenticating centre of New Testament doctrine. Scripture cannot of itself produce *the*, or even *a*, christian tradition: it can only be lived and understood within and according to a christian tradition. For all its great value, protestantism is a limited christian tradition: owing largely to its historical origins it has very heavily emphasised the written and spoken word as the almost exclusive medium of God's self-communication, and of christian meaning and self-expression.

As a careful and theoretical answer to the question about the criterion of christian truth, *sola scriptura* will not do. First of all, one must say, because there is no such thing: there is only scripture within and interacting with a living christian tradition. Secondly, because scripture by itself does not answer the questions that arise: all views, all heresies, all divisions, have based themselves on scripture, from the early christological controversies onwards. And scripture cannot answer questions which its writers did not ask and could not have asked, whether the questions put in the second century by Greek philosophy about the being of Christ, or those put in the twentieth about over-population. One has to note that protestantism has throughout its history until the ecumenical movement of this century proved something of a divisive force, and has had on its hands an enduring problem of authority. The 'protest' element should exist as a constant and challenging factor within the Church; it is not meant to exist on its own. Nor was it meant to by Martin Luther.

The Report of the Anglican-Lutheran International Conversations states that: 'The Anglican and Lutheran Churches ... are at one in accepting the Holy Scriptures of the Old and New Testaments as the sufficient, inspired, and authoritative record and witness, prophetic and apostolic, to God's revelation in Jesus Christ.'[17] All would agree that the New Testament is the authoritative and inspired record of the Christ-event, and witness to the understanding of that event in the 'apostolic age'. It is the sufficient and only witness and record in these respects. It provides the essential foundation of later witness. But it cannot be the sufficient witness to all the Church's understanding of God's revelation in Jesus Christ in all ages of the Church. And it does not follow that one or other understanding of this revelation that came later in the Church cannot become authoritative and normative; nor that such later understandings can only be understandings of scripture. Prayer for the dead, and the understanding of the Eucharist in terms of change and of sacrifice, appear to be elements that became established in the Church at an early date (and without controversy), as part of her whole self-understanding and not simply as the result of reflection on texts recognised as holy scripture. Theology, and thus doctrine, are always attempts to express the present, living experience of the believing Church – guided, certainly, and nourished by scripture. They can never be simply a conceptual analysis of words.

The long and very interesting series of conversations between Roman Catholic and Lutheran theologians in America grasped the nettle by facing as a first topic the status of the Nicene Creed as a dogma ('dogma' being understood as authoritative and definitive doctrine). Here, of course, there is question of interpreting scripture, but in view of questions put to the Church in post-apostolic times. The two sets of theologians were able to reach a joint statement, in seven paragraphs, which include the following:

6) As we reflect upon the role of dogma in our separated communities, we are aware of the following:

(a) The Nicene Faith possesses a unique status in the hierarchy of dogmas by reason of its testimony to and celebration of the mystery of the Trinity as revealed in Christ Our saviour, and by reason of its *definitive reply to an ever-recurring question* [my italics]. This does not imply that the Nicene Faith exhausted the richness of Scripture regarding the person of Christ....

(b) We are agreed that authoritative teaching in the Church serves the people of God by protecting and nurturing the Faith. Dogma has a positive and a negative function. It authoritatively repudiates erroneous teaching, and asserts the truth as revealed in the saving deeds of God and in his gifts to his Church and to his world.

(c) The way in which doctrine is certified as dogma is not identical in the two communities, for there is a difference in the way in which mutually acknowledged doctrine receives ecclesiastical sanction.[18]

(d) Different understandings of the movement from kerygma to dogma obtain in the two communities. Full inquiry must therfore be made into two topics: first, the nature and structure of the teaching authority of the Church; and, secondly, the role of Scripture in relation to the teaching office of the Church.[19]

Finally, in considering the dictum *sola scriptura,* we must take note of the claim that is sometimes made, that scripture imposes itself by its own inner authority as the sole source for us today of revelation and of faith. This does not give an adequate ground for faith, as the treatment at the beginning of this book, relying partly on an earlier treatment, has endeavoured to show. By leaving out the living Church, it endangers the true fullness of the doctrine of the Incarnation. Nor is it true to the normal experience of being born and growing up within a christian community. What is true about the dictum, understood more as a warning, is that after the formation of the canon, scripture is pre-eminent above the statements of Councils and all other forms of self-expression in the Church and continues to challenge the Church's doctrines, defined and undefined, throughout history.

For all of the reasons so far given in these reflections on *sola scriptura*, the catholic theological tradition has seen the need to assert that there is authority within the Church herself to interpret the Gospel (man's grasp of God's self-communication in Christ) in the light of the new questions that continually arise in the Church's historical experience. Though it is difficult to separate the two questions, we are not here concerned with the manner in which such an authoritative interpreting power might manifest itself and be exercised (this will be considered in the next chapter), but with what theological criterion such an authority can and should use. Does catholic theology answer Luther's question? Is 'scripture in the light of tradition' a satisfactory answer?

One ground for dissatisfaction with this answer could be expressed in the question 'scripture in the light of *what* tradition?' For, if the word 'tradition' in the strict sense be reserved for the living divine-human process by which the Body of Christ hands on the Body of Christ then, in the expression 'scripture in the light of tradition', the word 'tradition' is being used to cover globally all the visible traces in history of the process. It covers all kinds of thought-processes and practices which are known to have flourished in the Church, including some that have been abandoned, including some that at least appear to conflict with each other. (For instance, the Church at a fairly early stage gave up expecting an imminent second Coming of Christ, and radically altered her self-understanding in the process.) As we have seen, scripture cannot by itself generate a single tradition, and it is obvious from history that it has not done so. And this inevitably raises the question whether all traditions are good traditions. Are all developments progress, or are some regress or deviation? And what would be the criterion for deciding? It seems that the only possible reply could be, 'scripture in the light of universally accepted tradition'. This would, of course, leave the question (for the next chapter), 'When is a tradition universally accepted?' Apart from these theoretical difficulties about 'scripture in the light of tradition' as the theological criterion we are seeking, history itself gives some warnings that cannot be ignored. Patristic theology remained very largely a commentary on scripture. The rationalism introduced by Anselm led further and further away from scripture, until eventually the scholastic theology which formed generations, even centuries, of catholic teaching, explained the Gospel primarily in terms of a highly developed thought-pattern drawn from the accepted philosophy, and quoted scripture spasmodically, appropriately and inappropriately, as proof texts for positions and ways of reasoning drawn from elsewhere. I am not here assuming that a theology that is somehow biblical is necessarily better than an unbiblical one. But two things followed from this procedure. One was, of course, that scripture was not always looked at squarely and listened to for what it actually says – though this must not be exaggerated: scripture, or at any rate the New Testament, continued to be meditated and to be preached in the liturgy, The other thing that followed was that a scholastic tradition began to propel itself uncontrolled. It created a tradition, which in the passing of time became *the* tradition. The norm of what the Church should teach became what the Church teaches. The tradition became its own norm, virtually self-sufficient, and remaining unchallenged until the revival of patristic scholarship in the nineteenth century and biblical in the twentieth. And this is the danger of 'scripture in the light of tradition'. The phenomenon now known to us as triumphalism emerged progressively: the Church as a sufficient norm to herself. The Spirit, after all, guides the Church. She is the Body of Christ, she is the immaculate Bride. She is one, holy, catholic, apostolic. All thought-patterns and observances she has adopted must be the choice of the Spirit.... One remembers what great hesitations there were on such grounds among some at Vatican II to allow that the Church had in any way erred or fallen short, or was sinful. Of course, what is wrong with this position is that the Church is not, in any absolute sense, one-holy-catholic-apostolic. This is what she constantly endeavours to become. Yet, because she is the Body of the Lord, these qualities or forces are essentially hers: she strives ever to become what she essentially is. Hence she needs to live in self-criticism, in openness to the Spirit. She will be nearer to the truth on her knees than on her throne, and must implore the Spirit without ceasing to guide her into all truth, to renew and reform her constantly,[20] to help her to face new problems and to find new answers. She cannot simply pluck the answers out of tradition, or traditions: or scripture.

So, is Luther answered? One has the impression that both catholic and protestant traditions have sought a type of answer that is not there to be found; an empirically decisive norm. The Church is indeed a sacrament of Christ's kingdom: not only a sign of his presence and action in history, but an effective sign conveying his presence and action. But not automatically a full or fully effective sign, regardless of how she lives. Certainly, the Spirit has always guided his Church, and so her history and her traditions are a witness to his guidance. But are they not also a witness to her infidelity? Has she ever responded perfectly to that guidance? Even in the writing of scripture?

Hence there is not, there cannot be, an empirically decisive theological norm or criterion for all christian truth. Scripture can only be interpreted in the light of tradition. Traditions must always be challenged and criticised in the light of scripture. The two norms must always be held in balance, in a lived tension, in what must always remain a search for, a guidance into, all truth.

That is not to say that Councils such as those at Nicea and Chalcedon do not represent definitive acquisitions. But the Church never faces the same question twice. All doctrines, and therefore all dogmas, are historically and culturally conditioned: the question asked is conditioned by the background against which it was asked. The question of free will has been put in many contexts. So, too, the question of the Trinity, of Christ, of the Eucharist, of original sin, of papal infallibility. What do Nicea, and Chalcedon, and Trent, and Vatican i, say to us today? The answers are not given by simply applying 'scripture in the light of tradition' or 'tradition in the light of scripture'. They are rather to be sought for, by applying both.

NOTES

1. See the article, *'Traditiones* in the Council of Trent', by M. Bévenot, SJ, *Heythrop Journal*, Vol IV (1963), pp 333-47.

2. 'Evangelium . . . tanquam fontem omnis et salutaris veritatis et morum disciplinae': Denzinger-Schonmetzer (D-S), 1501. *Mores* means custom, customary observances.

3. '(Synodus) perspiciensque hanc veritatem et disciplinam contineri in libris scriptis et sine scripto traditionibus, quae ab ipsius Christi ore ab apostolis acceptae aut ab ipsis apostolis Spiritu Sancto dictante quasi per manus traditae ad nos usque pervenerunt' (ibid).

4. See Bévenot, loc. cit.

5. See Piet Fransen, SJ, 'Unity and Confessional Statements', in *The Dublin Papers on Ecumenism*, Manila University, 1972.

6. By Vatican I 'faith' had acquired the narrower sense of 'doctrines'. In quoting Trent, Vatican I appears to have mistakenly given *mores* its own sense of 'morals', as the speakers did not have access to the fully edited Acts of Trent and so misunderstood Trent on this point. But neither Council lends support to the view that the Church has special guidance or authority to pronounce on 'morals' as an area separable from 'faith'—ie to make authoritative statements that are simply ethical and not an unfolding of insight drawn from revelation and beyond the reach of merely moral judgment.

7. The wording *partim contineri in libris scriptis partim sine scripto traditionibus* was changed, and *partim . . . partim* was replaced by *et*. See Yves Congar, OP, *Tradition and Traditions*, London, Burns and Oates, 1966, p 165.

8. D-S, 1507.

9. *in rebus fidei et morum ad aedificationem doctrinae pertinentium.* Once more, there is no distinction between faith and morals. The word *pertinentium* qualifies *morum*, not *rebus*. The distinction is drawn between customs that have a bearing on faith and those that do not.

10. For full exposition and documentation see Congar, op. cit. His diagram of uses of the word 'tradition' (p 307) shows the complexities and ambiguities the word had taken on in the course of the discussion.

11. The *Constitution on Divine Revelation* of Vatican II (n 8) glimpses this truth but perhaps does not focus it fully. 'Now what was handed on by the apostles includes everything which contributes to the holiness of life and the increase in faith of the People of God; and so the Church, in her teaching, *life* and worship, perpetuates and *hands on to all generations all that she herself is*, all that she believes' (my italics). This passage, and paragraphs 7-9 of the *Constitution* as a whole, hover between regarding what is handed on as a message and as a life; hence between regarding the process by which it is handed on as a conceptual and verbal process (preaching and teaching) and as a whole way of life.

12. Chapter III, section (a).

13. *The Theology of Revelation*, p 129.

14. Page 32.

15. Above, pp 33-4.

16. O. Cullmann, *La Tradition*, Neuchâtel and Paris, Delachaux et Niestlé, 1953.

17. *Anglican–Lutheran International Conversations*, London, SPCK, 1973, n 17.

18. Note, however, that there is agreement that it does receive such sanction.

19. *The Status of the Nicene Creed as Dogma of the Church*, Washington, National Catholic Welfare Conference, 1965.

20. 'Christ summons the Church, as she goes her pilgrim way, to that continual reformation of which she always has need, in so far as she is an institution of men here on earth. Therefore, if the influence of events or of the times has led to deficiencies in conduct, in Church discipline, or even in the formulation of doctrine (which must be carefully distinguished from the deposit of faith itself), these should be appropriately rectified at the proper moment.' Vatican II, *Decree on Ecumenism*, 6.

Chapter Six

TEACHING OFFICE IN THE CHURCH

(a) 'Magisterium'

The word *magisterium* means office or function of teaching.
Irenaeus writes of the apostles handing on to their successors
locum sui magisterii[1]: does this mean 'their position of
teaching' or 'the see of their teaching'? The word itself
does not seem to have been much used in the christian
literature of the west. It is only in the nineteenth century
that it emerges, spelt with a capital 'M', for the special role
in teaching of the bishops and as something shared by no one
else. Probably the usage was helped by the growing claim of
the Church of Rome to be *mater et magistra*. Thus, Innocent
III, in 1199, writes of the Church of Rome that, *quasi magis-
tram et matrem ceteris praeeminere*.[2] By Lateran IV in 1215
he has dropped the *quasi*: the Abbot Joachim is required to
profess that he holds the faith that is held by the Roman
Church, which, as the Lord provided, is the *mater et magistra*
of all the faithful.'[3] At Florence in 1439 the Pope in person,
and no longer the local Church of Rome, is *omnium christ-
ianorum patrem et doctorem*.[4]

But of course it is not simply a matter of a word. The idea
that there is authority vested in the Church's leaders to
settle matters of doctrine is as old as 'the Council of Jerusalem'
in Acts 15[5]: and what could be more basic to the Church's
self-understanding than the question whether it was or was
not under the Law? The idea developed in the Church into
that of local and ecumenical or universal councils. But the
recent emergence of the term *magisterium*, and then *sacred
magisterium*, within catholicism in a restrictive sense, has
had the unfortunate effect of suggesting that the teaching
function in the Church, as distinct from authoritative teach-

ing office, is restricted to the college of bishops with the Pope at their head.

Such a restriction cannot be supported theologically. Christ is the Rabbi, the Teacher, and teaching function is part of the gift of his own 'apostleship', or mission or sending by the Father, which he gives to the whole Church. It is primarily oriented towards teaching Christ to the world; but to fulfil this function the christian community must first be instructed itself. As early as First Corinthians we have evidence (12: 28) of 'teachers' as having a special gift of the Spirit in and for the Church: they are placed third to apostles (missionaries to the non-Christian) and prophets (roughly, preachers). So, too, in Romans 12: 4-8 where, as in 1 Tim 3: 12 and 5: 17, the function of teaching is distinguished from that of the pre-siding elders. In both First Corinthians and Romans the body metaphor is used in this context, and the point is that different members exercise different functions, and all need each other.

Nor is any restriction of teaching function to bishops at all true to history. Many of the Teachers of the Church (*doctores ecclesiae*) are lay people (Justin and the early Apologists) and they include Teresa of Avila. Many are priests, such as Jerome, John of the Cross. And of course Thomas Aquinas became a Teacher of the Church not because he was a priest but because he was recognised by the Church as its master theologian. The Church names as *doctores* those who have in fact taught the Church: it is not an office, but the post-factum recognition of a service. Of men like Athanasius, Augustine, John Chrysostom it can be said that they were made bishops because they were recognised as great teachers, rather than vice versa. In the Middle Ages the universities came to be recognised as the centres of christian doctrine: Albert the Great, made a bishop because of the renown he had gained as a teacher, resigned from administration after two years in order to return to *magisterium*. Aquinas wrote his *Opusculum Contra Impugnantes* to vindicate the right of the Friars, against the Paris establishment, to teach in the university. In all ages the theologians have been the leading teachers in the Church, and not least at Vatican II.

But we have started in the wrong place. The most important teachers in the Church are our mothers and fathers. Without the christian home there would be no People. And few popes and bishops would have become priests without the teaching of their mothers. In Augustine and Monica the basic truth gets classic recognition. And in the wake of parents there follow a host of school teachers, always to some extent *in loco parentis*, and a host of priests.

In other words, the teaching function of Christ is given to his whole people, to be shared diversely, indeed by all, in one role or another. And, as Paul rubbed in to the Corinthians, if anyone has a special gift in this direction, he or she would do well to remember that the whole Body needs all the gifts given to them all. Any special office or responsibility for teaching must be understood within this whole spectrum.

(b) *The teaching office of bishops*

In episcopal Churches it is part of the office and responsibility of the bishop in his diocese, or of the episcopal conference (college) in a region, to see that the Gospel is taught and soundly taught. This is part of their pastoral office as representatives of Christ the one Shepherd and Teacher.

It is to be hoped that many popes and bishops will be found who can speak with great spiritual authority – indeed, that many will be chosen for office because they can be seen to have this gift, this charisma. But such a gift is not part of the office as such, nor conferred by ordination to it. Nor should the use of such a phrase as *sacred magisterium* be allowed to create a picture of episcopal teaching function 'from above downwards', as if it were the role of bishops to teach the rest of the Church a faith it would otherwise not know. Nor, finally, is it any part of the office as such that bishops should be leaders of thought, initiators of new means of discovering and communicating meaning in the Gospel, specially endowed to assist true progress in the development of doctrine or to meet the new challenges, intellectual or otherwise, of an age.

There remains only one Shepherd and Teacher in the Church – Christ. Only one *magisterium* or teaching authority *par excellence* – Christ's. Episcopal office within a Church that is a sacrament of Christ's kingdom and kingship, is itself a sacrament of Christ, a sign of the One Teacher in his representatives. But not automatically a fully effectual sign. Episcopacy will be a fuller and more effective sign the more it draws out and supports the full *magisterium* or teaching function entrusted by Christ to the whole Church, the more it encourages all in the Church to exercise their own gifts and roles – parents, teachers of many kinds, priests, scholars. The role and responsibility of episcopacy as such within this process is the eventual one of sifting, assembling, authenticating – in so far as the process does not do this for itself. Paul wrote to the Thessalonians, to the whole congregation: 'Do not stifle inspiration, and do not despise prophetic utterances, but bring them all to the test and keep what is good in them and avoid what is bad of whatever kind.'[6] And in Roman Catholicism, as it officially acknowledges that the Spirit dwells in and inspires other christian communions,[7] what they or their members wish to assert on any of the questions of the hour has to be taken into serious consideration.

Of course, this whole spectrum of varied gifts among Christians, and the learning and teaching process that emerges from it, is not simply a matter of doctrine or of theology in any narrow and technical sense. There is also the whole process of moral assessment, of developing insight into human values, that continues among Christians; there is the question of interpersonal relations, and how the Church should live her own life; there are the many questions about how she should fulfil her mission to the world, etc. Sometimes a remarkable gift is given for the Church to an individual, perhaps a layman. Such was Francis of Assisi: and it was for those holding office in the Church to recognise and accept the Spirit's gift and thus to make it fruitful so as to revivify the Gospel in the Church.

The role of episcopacy as office, of *magisterium* as office, can thus be seen to be a balance, difficult to maintain, between encouragement and conservation. A role of eventual sifting and authenticating presupposes the encouraging of individuals in their own roles, in order that there may be a full witness to assess. But at the end of the day, preferably as long a day as possible, it is the responsibility of bishops to ensure the 'tradition' or handing on of the same reality, the same Gospel once given to the saints. In fulfilling this task they are a 'rule' for the faithful, and are themselves under a rule, namely the theological criterion for christian truth which we discussed in the last chapter. Scholastic theology expressed the situation as follows: hierarchic authority is a *regula* for the faithful in their profession of faith, but a *regula regulata et mensurata* by the message of God expressed in scripture and catholic tradition.[8] But we have seen that scripture and tradition do not provide any simple, easily applicable 'rule of thumb'. Hence one goes deeper in asserting that the 'rule' for teaching office in the Church is Christ himself, and that the office of teaching is a service of Christ the one Teacher – but of Christ as he dwells in and gives his life to the whole Church. Any such office needs some sort of constitutional or legal definition. But it is not in itself a constitutional reality brought into being by the law. Rather, constitutional law can only roughly indicate its inner spiritual reality, which is sacramental; for the Church is no merely human society. Episcopacy is a call and a charge from God the Father to be an effective sign of Christ in the community and communion of his Spirit.

(c) *Infallibility and indefectibility*

There is some agreement today between Roman Catholics and others that 'infallibility' is an unfortunate word. Perhaps more so in English than in Latin, as in our language it suggests the theologically quite irrelevant idea of some fount of instant and comprehensive wisdom. It is in fact a negative concept, denoting that God saves his Church from falling into serious error; not a positive one, suggesting that he guarantees her total grasp, all the time, of the whole truth. Because of the overtones of 'infallibility' and the many misapprehensions that surround the word, many christian theologians prefer the word 'indefectibility' – though in Latin the two words amount to two ways of saying the same thing, 'unable to fail'.

If, however, the word 'indefectible' is meant to convey that the Church, because guaranteed by the Lord's promise and indwelling (Mt 28: 20), is unable to fall away totally from her *faith*, but she is able substantially to fail in her *teaching*, then the one word will not do for the other; the word 'infallibility' would have to be kept to assert God's guidance of the Church in her teaching. For it was in the context of sending his disciples to make disciples of all nations, baptising them and teaching them, that Christ's promise was made (Mt 28: 19-20). And a Church which remained firm in her faith but did not manifest this firmness in her expression of it, would be unintelligible. If the Spirit guides the Church as a historical People, then there must be traces of that guidance in history.

The classic meaning of 'indefectibility' was always more than that of the Church not failing in faith, not ceasing to exist, not substantially losing its nature or failing in its job; it included reliability in teaching. Hence, if indefectibility is given this classic and ample sense, infallibility in teaching is within and part of it.[9] A long tradition lies behind the doctrine expressed by Aquinas that 'it is impossible that the judgement of the universal Church should err in matters of faith[10]: but to the concept of universality a vertical as well as a horizontal dimension must be given, and a sufficient duration of time allowed for.

This being so, it might seem a tenable position that, given a longish span of time, the official Church may indeed err, but will sooner or later right herself. This view of indefectibility has been well expressed by Professor Mascall in reply to a paper of my own. He writes: 'There is, I think, a valid, though as with all analogies an imperfect, analogy between the guidance of the Church in its life and teaching by the Holy Spirit and the cybernetic mechanisms which are such an important feature of modern technology and are a built-in feature of all living organisms, including man. That is to say, the Church is not prevented from divagations from the central path of right development and progress, but, when the divaga-

tions occur, they are corrected, usually at the cost of divagations in an opposite direction which need to be corrected in
their turn. The divagations may sometimes be large and to all
appearances catastrophic, but complete catastrophe never
occurs; the car which is the Church may sometimes swerve
wildly but it never in fact ends up in the ditch.[11] But how, in
the case of the Church, is one to know which are (or were) the
divagations, and which is (or was) 'the central path of right
development and progress'? On such a view, it would appear,
nothing is ever settled. Yet the general acceptance by the
Churches today of the early Councils shows an awareness
among them that the Church has the power to settle at any
rate some central questions. In earlier chapters we have seen
that this power in the Church does not come into being or
come into force only after the apostolic age: it starts on the
day of Pentecost; there is one gift of the indwelling Spirit,
enabling men to grasp and proclaim the Gospel, to see their
faith reflected in what their forebears wrote, and so eventually
to 'canonise' its expression, and thereafter both to be guided
and challenged by the New Testament and to interpret it by
the way the faith is lived. And this power argues something
more than indefectibility in Mascall's sense. It argues, not
necessarily an uninterrupted reliability in doctrine but, in
addition to an ultimate reliability, some means of knowing
when the Church is reliable. If the word 'infallibility' is un-
acceptable to denote this concept, because suggesting too
much, then perhaps 'ultimate reliability' or simply 'reliability'
will do. But it must include the notion of 'definition' of
doctrine, ie dogma. The word *definire* means that a limit is
somewhere, sometimes, set to discussion on some things, and
a point at issue determined; and so, in the course of the
Church's doctrinal development there can be such 'definitive'
acquisitions – not necessarily 'perfect' formulations of truth,
but formulations that guide further though and cannot be
simply set aside.[12]

There cannot, of course, be such things as perfect formulations. Any formulation of christian faith in words, including
those of scripture, suffers very considerable limitations. First
because of the subject-matter, the mystery of God's self-com-

munication in Christ, which can never be adequately grasped or exhausted by human minds, nor deployed without remainder into human statements. Secondly, because all human statements are historically, culturally and contextually conditioned.[13] Dr Hans Küng is therefore barking up the wrong tree in his assertions that Vatican I put forward a doctrine of *a priori* infallible propositions:[14] Vatican I neither launched a peculiar epistemology nor predicated infallibility of statements, but of persons. But he is basically right about the more general philosophical presuppositions at the time of Vatican I: the cartesian or camera-like view of the role of concepts and statements as perfectly mirroring reality, which therefore attributed to accepted formulas a timelessness and an adequacy they cannot possess. Yet our limited powers of statement are all we have got. And Küng's total relativising of all human statements would make it impossible for the Church, or indeed for anyone else, ever to state the simplest truths and to make definitively reliable statements. To say that a statement is reliable and definitive in the sense explained is not to say it is the best possible statement of the reality being considered; nor that it says all there is to say; nor that it uses timeless words. Indeed, to say that a statement is guaranteed by infallibility is not of itself to say that it is a particularly important statement – only that it is definitive and reliable.

As is well known, Vatican I defined that the Pope is infallible when he speaks *ex cathedra*, 'that is, when in discharge of the office of pastor and doctor of all Christians, by virtue of his supreme apostolic authority he defines a doctrine regarding faith or morals to be held by the universal Church'. But this statement does not determine the precise scope and subject-matter of infallibility, ie the limits of what in the areas of faith and morals is *divinely revealed*; and so this has remained a debated question. Vatican I intended to produce a *Constitution on the Church*, but was abruptly ended by the Franco-Prussian war and never did so, though its document dealing only with the papacy still bore the title, 'Dogmatic Constitution on the Church of Christ'. Hence, in defining papal infallibility the Council said that the Pope has 'that infallibility with which the divine Redeemer wished his Church to be endowed'.[15] The phrase was not intended to convey (or to exclude) the idea that the Pope is the mouthpiece of the Church, but to assert that the scope of infallibility was the same in each case and to leave open to later determination what that scope was.[16] In the body of the Constitution the statement occurs: 'For the Holy Spirit was not promised to Peter's successors in order that by his revelation they might make known new doctrine, but that with his assistance they might keep in sacred trust and faithfully expound the revelation delivered through the apostles, the deposit of faith.'[17] The general tenor of this sentence is clearly restrictive but, especially in view of theories of development of doctrine current at the time, the expression '*expound* the revelation....' leaves some uncertainty about scope. An unfortunate result of the Council's not completing its work of defining (and thus limiting) the scope of infallibility was that it opened the way to what has come to be called 'creeping infallibility', at least in the popular mind. Many Roman Catholic theologians, then and now, would wish to limit the possible subject-matter of infallible pronouncements to matters seen to be so central to the Church's faith as to be called *stantis et cadentis ecclesiae*, and thus to involve the central fidelity of God to his covenant and promises. For the doctrine of infallibility is basically about God's promise and protection, not about man's powers. Others would limit the scope to matters arising directly out of the interpretation of scripture.[18] Vatican II's *Constitution on the Church* states the scope of infallibility as follows: 'It is commensurate with the deposit of divine revelation, which is to be kept in sacred trust and faithfully expounded.'[19] It must first be noted that Vatican II was not itself 'defining' the scope of infallibility in the strict dogmatic sense. It will also be noted that here Vatican II repeats the statement of Vatican I just quoted above, but with some modifications. It avoids, as does the *Constitution on Divine Revelation*, the expression 'deposit of faith', possibly because this latter expression tends to suggest an original list of doctrines, and speaks instead of 'the deposit of divine revelation'. But this, too, is unclear. Presumably, if a list of doctrines is not intended, either the Christ-events themselves or the meaning of the Christ-events as grasped in the apostolic age is meant. But the only evidence for either is the New Testament, and so one might conclude that in-fallibility does not go beyond the interpretation of scripture. However, the statement also preserves from Vatican I the phrase 'to be faithfully expounded', which still leaves un-certainty about whether doctrines that manifestly developed after the apostolic age, even though somehow based in scrip-ture, are included in the scope of infallibility.

It remains true that the thrust of the two passages is restrictive: the guidance of the Spirit is not for the promul-gation of any new doctrine; the scope of infallibility goes no further than the revelation entrusted to the apostles; the word 'deposit' suggests an original and limited body of truth, beyond which God's special protection does not extend. Hence one can safely conclude that a doctrine cannot become a doc-trine of faith by being defined authoritatively; rather, only doctrines of original and basic faith can be authoritatively defined.

(d) *When does the Church teach reliably?*

The Orthodox tradition exhibits and holds fast to the fact that one can only believe, and not prove, that the Church is able to teach with definitive reliability; it goes further and maintains that it can only be a matter of faith *when* the Church is in fact so teaching. For the Orthodox, an ecumenical council teaches definitively, but it is only post factum and *ex consensu ecclesiae* that a council is known to be ecumeni-cal: if and in so far as its teaching is accepted as a true ex-pression of the Church's faith, then the council is seen to be ecumenical. This would align authoritative Church teaching with the process by which the New Testament came to be canonised: ie just as it is the gradual and eventually firm acceptance of these writings by the Church that gives them canonical status, and makes them holy scripture, so with conciliar statements.

One difficulty with this position is that, if a large body of Christians such as the Arians or Nestorians do not in fact accept the teaching of the council, can you ever say that it has acquired the consent of the Church? No doubt the Orthodox would reply that it always remains a matter of faith, not of any firm empirical criterion; one believes that the Church spoke, and spoke reliably, at Nicea, at Chalcedon. Yet the argument might be pressed further: the sign of the Church's consent can be discerned when the dissident bodies are relatively small, but what if doctrinal issues split the Church into large bodies that continue to exist with counter-claims? Perhaps in logic the answer should be that then Christians must work for a reconciling council, whose voice would in time come to be seen as that of the Church, and that only such a council could decide the issues. But in fact they have maintained that their own tradition is decisive.

Other difficulties with the theory arise from the facts of history. For instance, Professor Frend has recently shown[20] that the Council of Chalcedon, so far from settling anything and receiving quasi-universal consent, launched two centuries of bitter division in which the 'Monophysites' or anti-Chalcedonians conquered such vast tracts of christian allegiance that they came in time to outnumber the pro-Chalcedonians. They were reduced to a small proportion, not by seeing the error of their ways, but by the Arab invasions. It would take a very hardy mind to see the Arabs in this instance as the hammer of God!

A further point that calls for reflection is the position in Orthodox tradition of the Ecumenical Patriarch. If I have understood the matter aright, the Orthodox Churches would not regard any council as ecumenical without the participation and/or consent of the Patriarch of Constantinople. If so, then the criterion, or process of recognition of the Church's reliability in doctrine is not purely the subsequent consent of the Church, and the Orthodox position may in its principles be nearer to the Roman Catholic than has generally been supposed: the consent of the Church needs a focus or centre.

By contrast Catholicism has come to hold an empirical criterion for the ecumenicity of a council: such a criterion would be external to whatever an ecumenical council might affirm; the council would be recognisable by an empirical criterion as ecumenical, and therefore its teaching would carry authority *ex sese* (from itself, because it was the authoritative voice), and not from subsequent recognition or acceptance by the Church as truly stating the Church's faith.

The empirical criterion proposed has, of course, been the position of the Bishop of Rome. There are, however, two ways of stating what is meant, a more legal and a more theological way. It could be said that the catholic tradition has come to affirm a constitutional criterion: that council is ecumenical which is ratified by the authority of the Pope. But theological insight is prior to any attempt to give it legal or constitutional expression, and, therefore, the theological way of stating the criterion is the fundamental one. Theologically the papacy can been seen as a sacramental sign of the unity and authority which Christ gives to his Church, a sign of Christ's *episcope* over the whole Church: a sacramental sign, hence both visible (or empirical) and effective. The criterion should then be stated thus: that council can be recognised as ecumenical which is a general council of bishops in communion with the See of Rome as their centre of unity.

The theological argument for so understanding the papacy and ecumenical councils is a long and complex one, covering the history of the idea from its first emergence in 343 at the Council of Sardica. It includes much discussion whether the councils which are commonly recognised by Christians as ecumenical themselves accepted the idea; what were the motives of those who appealed to Rome as arbiter, or rejected such an appeal, etc. It is not possible to enter here into the details of the argument. Rather should we stand back from it and consider its nature.

It is an argument within the understanding of scripture and tradition that has been proposed in these pages, and hence it sees no difficulty in principle in the idea that the Church should come to understand herself in the course of history, under the guidance of the Holy Spirit, as local Churches in communion through their bishops with the See of Rome; and hence come to accept that a council in communion with the Pope spoke authoritatively for the Church. The crux of the matter must be whether the Church did so come to understand itself. It is the kind of argument that seeks to establish what is the faith of the Church about herself; what is the consensus within, and self-understanding of, the Church. The Orthodox tradition will, of course deny that this is its understanding of the Church; Catholicism will assert it. But it is surely important for us to see that in either case the ultimate appeal is to the faith of the Church.

Let us put the matter another way. Why, at the end of the day, when the dust of argument has settled, do Roman Catholics believe that Trent and Vatican I were ecumenical councils? Because they were general councils of bishops in communion with the See of Rome. Why, then, do Catholics accept that that is what makes a council ecumenical? Not ultimately on the strength of the historical and theological arguments: they might pardonably find these inconclusive; their grounds for belief would then be no firmer than the arguments themselves; and the vast majority of Roman Catholics know nothing of the arguments anyway. No, they believe it; they believe within a Church; they share the faith of a Church, and this is their ultimate ground. And so, surely, do others in other Churches.

Must not Catholics and Orthodox, then beneath their differences, be appealing ultimately to the same principle, the consent of the Church as to its faith, in this case to its self-understanding? Practice, or experience, precedes theory in the Church's life; theology is a thematisation of experience. Orthodoxy and Catholicism have experienced the nature of the Church differently over the centuries. All I wish to suggest is that they have more of a common basis in their understanding of the process of revelation than has generally been recognised; and hence that they could work for a mutual consensus from this basis. The idea of (subsequent) 'consent' of the Church may be too legal a way of expressing the Orthodox experience of recognition and acceptance of a council as ecumenical, just as 'papal ratification' is too legal a way of expressing Catholic experience. Both traditions accept the idea of a growing self-understanding in the Church under the guidance of the Spirit and under the norm of scripture. The ultimate ground in both for accepting an authoritative voice is 'consensus', the way the Church has come to experience the Church.

(e) *Ordinary teaching office*

The ordinary *magisterium* of the Pope and bishops is another area in this complex field. To assert that the ordinary teaching of the bishops is a reliable guide to christian truth is primarily to assert that God is faithful to his promises, and that episcopacy is the sure sign of this enduring care by Christ, the one Shepherd and Teacher. It is also to indicate a fact, that the bishops at any given time corporately reflect and manifest the current doctrinal expression of the Church's faith and are regarded as doing so reliably by the faithful.

In 1950 Pius XII defined the doctrine of the Assumption of Our Lady, as part of the long accepted Catholic faith, after direct written consultation with all the Catholic bishops. This was a historically unique case of the current belief and teaching of the bishops being given formal expression outside a general council. The doctrine was not a matter of controversy or dispute in Catholicism. But on any controversial matter, such as one arising from new perspectives or new questions, it would in practice be impossible to know without conciliar processes what the true mind of the bishops was. This was exemplified at Vatican II, during which the debates showed many divergences of view. And Vatican II's doctrinal statements (which it did not regard as definitive or dogmatic in the technical sense) reveal at many points compromise formulae intended to keep a debate open and not to end it. Nor would theologians understand 'ordinary' teaching simply in terms of accepted current teaching, even if there were means for determining this. To believe in the doctrinal reliability of the ordinary teaching of bishops does not entail belief that their current teaching, if it could be adequately assessed, would at all points be irreversible; it does not ex-

clude periods of greater and periods of more limited understanding. 'Ordinary teaching' is too loose a concept to use
as a definitive guide. Only the eventual, and perhaps continual, assessment process by the Church (the consensus of
the Church once more) could establish what the ordinary
teaching is. This is the element of universality taken in its
full sense.[21] Finally, Roman Catholic theology needs to be
more aware that it cannot at the same time insist on the
ordinary teaching of bishops as a reliable guide, and ignore
the teaching of leaders in other Churches who are recognised
to be true bishops. Indeed, one must look beyond episcopacy,
if the assertion of the *Decree on Ecumenism* that the Holy
Spirit operates in other christian bodies is to be taken
seriously. Only an exclusivist view of the centrality of the
Roman Catholic Church could regard the witness of other
christian Churches and leaders as simply irrelevant to matters
of christian truth under discussion.

The ordinary teaching of the Pope, in the form of an
encyclical or similar pronouncement, certainly carries for
Roman Catholics an authority *ex sese*, an authority that must
be first described as spiritual authority. Papal statements will
attract more notice and respect, they will enter more fully
into discussion, than the statements of another bishop or
group of bishops. But as a matter of historical fact, their ultimate doctrinal value can be seen to be subject to a process of
subsequent assessment, which could be described as *ex consensu ecclesiae*, a process to which it is not possible to place
any particular term. One might take as examples the 1864
Syllabus of Errors of Pius IX or the social encyclical *Rerum
Novarum* of Leo XIII. Both attracted a good deal of attention
from teachers and thinkers in the Church. Both entered for
long afterwards, and perhaps still do, into the 'authorities',
the doctrinal statements of importance, considered by theologians. But the place they will eventually take within the
doctrinal self-expression of the Church, their ultimate doctrinal authority, can only progressively be discerned in the
Church's long, and perhaps unending, process of assessment.

That is not to say that a papal pronouncement cannot
require the assent of true faith. But this will depend on its

subject-matter. It will require the assent of faith if and because it treats of a matter of faith revealed by God, and expresses the faith of the Church, not because it is an act of the Pope's ordinary *magisterium*. And here at this very central point is an undecided issue in catholic theology, affecting the whole exercise of *magisterium*, papal or episcopal, ordinary or extraordinary. Can the authoritative voice in the Church determine that particular matters are matters of divine revelation by decreeing them to be so? Or must there not be a theological method, independent of the organs of proclamation, for deciding the scope and therefore the limits of what is divinely revealed? This is precisely the question of the scope of infallibility left undetermined by Vatican i.

(f) *Extraordinary teaching office of the Pope*

And so we come at last, and only against this complex background, to the infallibility of the Pope. We have to recall all that has been said about the co-extensiveness of the Pope's and the Church's teaching authority in the documents of Vatican i and ii, and also the necessary limitations of any human statements.

In addition, the point needs to be made that at Vatican i the adjective 'infallible' was applied not to the dogmatic statements of the Pope, but to the Pope himself: the statements are called *irreformabiles*. There was, however, no assertion of special guidance by the Holy Spirit of the Pope's thinking outside the act of defining; nor do the phrases *charisma veritatis* and *assistentia divina*[22] require any such idea. Indeed, in the article already referred to Fr Congar recalls the notable speech of Cardinal Guidi which secured two textual alterations in Vatican i's Constitution, to avoid affirming this. Guidi insisted that the Pope was not personally infallible by some inherent and enduring power or gift, but only by transient assistance and protection in the act of defining. The word 'infallible' qualifies the person in the act of judgement by which he pronounces. As a result of this speech, the title of the relevant chapter 4 of the Constitution was changed from *De Romani Pontificis Infallibilitate* (of the Pope's infallibility) to *De Romani Pontificis Infallibili Magisterio* (of the Pope's infallible teaching). And the definition itself was so worded as to say, '*when the Pope defines*, he has, by the divine assistance, that infallibility with which the divine Redeemer wished his Church to be endowed'. It does not follow that the Pope at other times has no special assistance from God in his acts of teaching; but it is not part of the doctrine of Vatican I that he has.

With all these provisos, then, we may now consider the simpler question whether, within the total teaching function of the Church, the papacy has a particular role to play as a sure sign of reliable teaching. The theological argument for accepting the idea is of the same kind as that for the criterion of the ecumenicity of a council: basically, that this understanding of the role of the papacy grew in Catholicism as an interpretation of the New Testament Petrine texts and gained common acceptance. In this case, however, there are exceptional historical difficulties. Recent studies[23] have shown that the specific idea of papal infallibility, within a more general idea of the doctrinal primacy of the See of Rome, emerged almost by accident in the course of non-doctrinal controversy from 1150 onwards; and that the theologians who supported it did so, partly mistakenly though *bona fide* on the basis of a collection of papal decrees (the False Decretals) that was in fact spurious, partly with the support of genuine documents. Thus was founded a theological tradition on partly false historical premises, and the doctrine was eventually defined after being in possession for some centuries on the basis of the existing tradition.

We shall not attempt to assess here the strength or weakness of the theological argument for the Pope's special position within the Church's power to speak authoritatively on the content of divine revelation. Rather we shall again try to stand back and to consider the nature or shape of the discussion. Once more, it is not in principle impossible for a doctrine concerned with the Church's self-understanding to emerge in the course of her history, though the historical basis of the doctrine would in this case remain disquieting.

But the argument in favour of the doctrine necessarily seeks to establish that, however late or piecemeal it emerged, it eventually became part of the accepted faith of the Catholic Church. And it necessarily presupposes, in this case, that the belief of Roman Catholicism is equivalent to the belief of the Church, though of course the Orthodox and Reformed Churches would not agree. Thus, as with the ecumenicity of councils, Catholics, whether theologians or not, believe in the Pope's special teaching office, not ultimately on the strength of the theological argument, but because they believe within their Church.

Let us again look at the point from another angle. Various logical difficulties can be raised about the idea of infallibility in doctrine.[24] One is aware of the danger of circularity in the notion of a Council defining that the Pope (in carefully stated circumstances) has that power of infallible teaching which the Church has, because the Church is here defining its own infallibility. In logic, one does not first have to accept the Church's infallibility in order to accept her pronouncement that she is infallible: for one might reach certainty by theological argument that she has the power of infallible pronouncement in matters of divine revelation, and one might reach conviction by theological argument that the nature of the Church herself was truly a matter of divine revelation. But even supposing one found such arguments quite convincing, to believe the conclusions with christian faith is something quite other than accepting the force of an argument; for this would entail reservation or rejection if one did not find the arguments conclusive; and it would imply that only thorough and convinced theologians have grounds for accepting the conclusion. The doctrines we have been considering in this chapter can only ultimately be *believed*, like any other christian doctrines. To believe is to share the faith of a christian community, to have encountered Christ and to be aware of his guiding presence in this community, in ways that have taken human form and expression.

I have laboured this point for two reasons. Firstly, because it seems to me to set doctrines about the Church's reliability in teaching within an understanding of the whole process of faith and revelation. But, secondly, these reflections seem to me to point to a way forwards in the present search for christian unity.

(g) *The state of the question*

A theme that has constantly recurred in this study is that of the *sensus fidelium* in various forms. It was Israel who knew who were her true prophets, speaking authentically to the core of her faith and challenging the 'establishment' of both court and cult; it was Israel who progressively made a classic of some of the inherited treasures of her religious literature; it was the apostolic community that was led by the Spirit to see itself as the Body of the Risen Lord, bringing Israel and its heritage to their true fullness, and which preached the Gospel as the 'filling full' of the Old Testament; it was the living and believing Church which slowly came to form and to select the New Testament as the classic expression of the apostolic faith. We have seen that the same factor is at work in the recognition of Fathers, Doctors, Councils. If that factor is called *consensus ecclesiae*, then it must be given the broad and deep sense of 'con-sensus', and not be imagined as some particular legal or constitutional act.[25] In a remarkable passage Vatican II spoke of the *sensus fidelium* as follows:

> The holy People of God shares also in Christ's prophetic office. It spreads abroad a living witness to him, especially by means of a life of faith and charity and by offering to God a sacrifice of praise, the tribute of lips which give honour to his name (cf Heb 13: 15). The body of the faithful as a whole, anointed as they are by the Holy One (cf John 2: 20, 27), cannot err in matters of belief. Thanks to a supernatural sense of the faith which characterises the People as a whole, it manifests this unerring quality when, 'from the bishops down to the last member of the laity' (Augustine, *De praedestinatione sanctorum*, 14, 27), it shows universal agreement in matters of faith and morals.[26]

We reflected at the beginning of this chapter that Christ gives

his teaching function to the whole Church to be variously
exercised and guided. The Council says explicitly that 'the
holy People of God shares in Christ's prophetic office'. It
would not be normal, or indeed helpful, to speak of the infallibility of the whole Church. But when the Council says
that the whole People shares in Christ's prophetic office, it
is saying more than that they have indefectibility in faith:
they manifest this unerring quality when they show universal
agreement. Hence the consensus of the Church enters into
the process by which the Church endeavours under God's
guidance to teach reliably. A weakness in Vatican ii's documents is that it treated ecumenism in one decree, and then
perhaps tended to overlook this dimension in others. A case
in point is the use of the phrase 'the People of God': in reading the *Constitution on the Church* one finds oneself wonder-
ing whether the phrase is meant to include or to exclude other
Christians. It cannot simply exclude them after such a statement as: 'It is the Holy Spirit, dwelling in those who believe,
pervading and ruling over the whole Church, who brings
about that marvellous communion of the faithful and joins
them together so intimately in Christ that he is the principle
of the Church's unity.'[27] Hence, whatever ecclesiological
model one may be using, and Vatican ii's documents use
several models,[28] the *sensus fidelium* of other Christians cannot simply be disregarded in evaluating the prophetic and
teaching process by which the Church expresses its faith.

The history of the Church's Councils shows that they have
been concerned with statements of faith that were seen as
necessary to preserve unity; they have tended towards the
minimal necessary statement for this purpose and have tried
to avoid the appearance of settling or limiting legitimate
theological discussion. I think it is fair to say that Protestantism, in witnessing to the primacy of scripture, has never fully
faced up to the question of the reliability of the Church's
understanding of scripture. It does not seem rash to assert
that the doctrine of the Church's reliability in teaching is
still in the process of development within Roman Catholicism: Catholic theologians today are wrestling with a number
of problems raised by the definition of Vatican i which were

beyond the horizons of discussion at that Council. On the other hand, Roman Catholicism and Orthodoxy seem nearer to each other on this question than has often been supposed, and yet neither in isolation from the other is capable of reaching an adequate self-understanding of the Church. I therefore see both the need and the possibility for these three great theological traditions to enter more fully into discussion with each other and move towards a common understanding. Out of it could grow a greater understanding of the nature and signs of God's guidance of the Church in her teaching than the christian people as a whole has ever yet attained.

NOTES

1. *Adv Haer*, 3.1.1.
2. D-S 774.
3. D-S 807.
4. D-S 1307.
5. Luke appears to have conflated in verses 6-29 of this chapter accounts of two separate occasions.
6. 1 Thess 5:19-22.
7. 'Nor should we forget that whatever is wrought by the Holy Spirit in the hearts of our separated brothers can contribute to our own edification.' Vatican II, *Decree on Ecumenism*, 4.
8. So Cajetan, *Comm in Summ Theol*, 2a-2ae, 1.1.
9. See the article by Yves Congar, OP, '*Infaillibilité et Indéfectibilité*', in *Revue de Sciences Phil et Theol*, 54 (1970), pp 601ff.
10. *Quodlibetum*, 9.16; further references in Congar, op. cit.
11. See *The Ampleforth Journal*, LXXVII (1972), p 46.
12. The term used to cover such statements in Vatican I's definition of papal infallibility is *irreformabiles*.
13. In addition, some of the realities about which the Church tries to express herself are themselves historically conditioned, eg her own ministry.
14. H. Küng, *Infallible ?*, London, Collins, 1971, pp 123-4 and subsequently throughout the book.
15. D-S 3074.
16. See Congar, op. cit.
17. D-S 3070: Neque enim Petri successoribus Spiritus Sanctus promissus est, ut eo revelante novam doctrinam patefacerent, sed ut, eo assistente, traditam per apostolos revelationem seu fidei depositum sancte custodirent et fideliter exponerent.
18. As long as the theological scope of infallibility remains undetermined, the question can continue to be raised about any particular statement whether it is in fact guaranteed by God, even if all external conditions of an infallible pronouncement are fulfilled.

19. *Lumen Gentium*, n 25: Haec autem infallibilitas ... tantum patet quantum divinae revelationis patet depositum.

20. W. H. C. Frend, *The Rise of the Monophysite Movement*, Cambridge University Press, 1972.

21. See section (c) above. This element is present in the famous *regula fidei* propounded by Vincent of Lerins (*Commonitorium*, 2) in the fifth century: *quod ubique, quod semper, quod ab omnibus creditum est*. But Vincent held a very diehard view of tradition, and his exposition and 'canon' in fact leave no room for any development of doctrine at all.

22. D-S 3071, 3074.

23. In particular: Yves Congar, op, *L'Ecclésiologie du Haut Moyen-Age*, Paris Editions du Cerf, 1968; Brian Tierney, *The Origins of Papal Infallibility 1150 to 1350*, Leiden, E. J. Brill, 1972.

24. Some of these are treated by Dr Patrick McGrath in his chapter, 'The Concept of Infallibility', in *Truth and Certainty*, ed E. Schillebeeckx and B. van Iersel, Herder and Herder, 1973.

25. Some reflections were made on the *sensus fidelium* in Chapter 4, section (a).

26. *Lumen Gentium*, 12.

27. *Decree on Ecumenism*, 2.

28. See the article by Avery Dulles, sj, 'The Church, the Churches, and the Catholic Church', in *Theological Studies*, 33 (1972), pp 199-234.

Chapter Seven

THE BIBLE IN THE CHURCH

(a) *The classical model of biblical theology*

A single basic attitude of mind to the interpretation of scripture, and a single basic method in theology, lasted in the
Church for a thousand years from Paul to Abelard (inclusive):
its greatest exponent was Origen, who gave it classical form.
This whole model of biblical theology has in our own day
been given superb exposition and documentation in the monu-
mental work of Henri de Lubac.[1]

Paul wrote to the Galatians (4: 22-24): 'It is written that
Abraham had two sons, one by his slave and the other by his
free-born wife. The slave-woman's son was born in the course
of nature, the free woman's through God's promise. This is
an allegory. The two women stand for two covenants....'
This passage gave the method its key idea and one of its key
words. It is not the Old Testament account that is an allegory,
but the people and the events themselves. Similarly Paul
wrote to the Corinthians (1 Cor 10: 1-11) a whole passage in
which he saw central events of Israel's religious experience as
types of what is central to christian faith: 'The rock was
Christ.... All these things happened to them symbolically
(*tupikōs*) and were recorded for our benefit as a warning.'

The basic assumption of the method, as it came to be worked
out in detail by Origen, was that all revelation was contained
in the Bible – indeed, all knowledge worth knowing: Plato's
wisdom could only be explained by some unrecorded influence
of Moses. The whole of theological science consisted in explaining scripture. Traditional insights were preserved and
handed on ('tradition' in this context means traditional understanding of scripture), because only the Spirit in the Church

can understand scripture aright. Development of doctrine meant a growing understanding of scripture. Abelard himself had no other aim than to provide for his students an understanding of the sacred page (*divinae paginae intelligentiam*).

Central to this patristic understanding of scripture is that there are basically two senses, the literal (or historical) and the spiritual (or mystical). The Old Testament gives the *letter*, the New Testament gives the *spirit*.

Revelation, in this view, took place in history, as events rather than as pronouncements: it is the real events that were 'mysterious', that both concealed and disclosed God. Hence there was a veneration for sacred history, for the history recorded in the Old Testament, but no interest in history for its own sake, for its human sake, no cultural interest, no concern with secular historical movements and patterns (as in Thucydides). History was a moral science, a tale of the *magnalia Dei*. It was therefore important to establish what happened, the literal sense, the letter. There was real 'scientific study, to achieve this, and it was not a matter of allegorising in the hellenic or pagan sense of replacing recorded events with patterns of ideas.[2] It was important to establish the literal sense in order to discern *its* spiritual sense, the christian message conveyed by what happened.

For the New Testament gave the spiritual (or mystical or allegorical) sense of the Old Testament events (this is precisely Paul's model). The Christian must not understand the Old Testament according to the letter, but according to its spirit, according to Christ, according to the New Testament. 'The whole mystery of all the scriptures is Christ and his Church'[3] wrote Augustine: he was not speaking of abstract ideas, but of the present and future *realities* of this world and of the next (as was Paul). The spiritual sense does not displace the literal sense but grows out of it, or is seen by the eye of christian faith beneath its surface. The spiritual sense is totally from inside the faith: it alone is the christian understanding of the Old Testament. The Word is now incarnate, and sheds his true light on the word of God in the Old Testament. Only Christians can truly understand the Old Testament. It is Christ, not a historical process open to secular inspection, that makes the two testaments one. 'The spirit of the letter itself is Christ,'[4] He, the *Logos*, interprets the Old Testament, not by explaining it but by fulfilling it. He brings the history of Israel to its consummation, to the fullness towards which it reached out. (The perspective is exactly that of the synoptic evangelists, most fully worked out in Matthew.) The Christ-event gives the meaning of God's acts in Israel's history. *Crede ut intellegas* (believe first in order to understand), wrote Augustine over and over again: it was precisely John's contrast between seeing materially and seeing spiritually.

The Church is the fulfilment of Israel – the true People, not a new People. The Church is *Israel secundum spiritum*. The only ultimately true sense of scripture is that given by the Spirit in the Church. Thus there became only one Testament for a Christian, only one point from which to read the message of God. Scripture was the Christian's spiritual reading: there was little need of treatises other than on scripture, little need of manuals or books of devotion.

In the fully articulated patristic 'method in theology' the mystical or spiritual sense was differentiated into three[5]: doctrinal, ascetical, anagogic. The whole and only point of doctrine was to nourish the spiritual life of Christians; ascetical understanding governed christian living, and opened out into the last (anagogic) stage of penetration of the mysteries of God, the (in the modern technical sense) mystical or in-prayer knowledge of God. So each of these distinctions within the spiritual sense is a step beyond the previous one leading further into the mystery. They are not a dividing up of the same ground, a parting of ways, but a breaking through into new horizons. Thus patristic theology had a true eschatology, lost to scholasticism: mystical understanding of the Church pointed to the future consummation; earthly and heavenly Church (*ouranios ekklesia*) were one reality: the City of God.

The system of course broke up with the revival of philosophy, introduced first as dialectic, or linguistic analysis, by Anselm and Abelard; and with the rediscovery of the value of knowledge gained by empirical observation. Mystery began to be unpacked into explanation, into reasoning, into the philosophical system. Theology set off on the long road of systematic conceptual explanation. *Doctrina* came to supersede *scriptura*. From the eleventh century a unity of culture dissolved.

(b) *The Old Testament as a christian book*

The *allegoria* or mystical understanding of the Fathers ran wild, and became discredited, because there were no theological criteria for what was a genuine 'spiritual sense', and what was sheer imagination, or more or less successful poetry. But their basic vision of the relation of Old and New Testaments, and of their becoming one Testament, the tradition of a thousand years, must surely stand. It can hardly be doubted by a christian theology, ie one speaking from within the christian faith and seeking to give it expression. It was revived in a few phrases of Vatican II's *Constitution on Divine Revelation*:

> God, the inspirer and author of both testaments, 'wisely arranged that the New Testament be hidden in the Old and the Old be made manifest in the New.' For, though Christ established the New Covenant in his blood (cf Lk 22:20; 1 Cor 11:25), still the books of the Old Testament with all their parts, caught up into the proclamation of the gospel, acquire and show forth their full meaning in the New Testament (cf Mt 5:17; Lk 24:27; Rom 16:25-26; 2 Cor 3:14-16) and in turn shed light on it and explain it.[6]

The patristic and early medieval ages, indeed, stressed the continuity between Old and New Testaments. There is continuity on the plane of history and culture. The religious genius of Israel is beyond question: its prayer, its religious vision and its leading religious concepts are taken up into christian life. The New Testament breathes the idiom of the Old. It brings its main themes and aspirations to fulfilment and carries them beyond themselves. One sentence of a ninth-century exegete captures this truth: 'What shines out in the Old Testament blazes forth in the New.'[7]

But there is far more stress on the discontinuity, on the complete break. 'Behold I make all things new' (Rev 21:5). Origen wrote of 'conversion (*metanoia*) from the letter to the spirit'.[8] Irenaeus: 'Bringing himself, he brought all newness.'[9] There is discontinuity and total newness at the central point of faith: God became man. This is what makes the idea of allegory in its patristic sense irreplaceable. In Christ there is a new creation: everything is radically transformed in him. In his death on the cross he puts to death the letter, the *umbras et imagines*; he penetrates the holy of holies and tears down the veil. The Fathers even compare Christ's accomplishment of the scriptures to the transformation that takes place in the Eucharist: the word is only nourishment for the Christian when consecrated by Christ.[10]

How, then, preserve this basic and essential christian vision, and yet find the theological criterion for deciding what is the christian sense of the Old Testament? It is not just a question for a speculating theologian. It is the crucial question for the preacher, every time he reads a passage of the Old Testament to his people. We call the Old Testament 'the word of God'. Is it? in its own right? for the christian preacher? Certainly the tradition of a thousand years did not think so.

Various modern theologians have written on this problem.[11] Professor Lohfink argues as follows: the Old Testament grew by constant addition and reformulation; the New Testament must be regarded as the last and definitive addition to the Old; only the whole Bible seen as one is 'inerrant' or the word of God addressed to the Christian; hence only a theology of the whole Bible is a truly biblical theology. But, he adds, such a presentation of the Bible does not yet exist.

It seems to me that it is Dodd who gives the basic clue to such a biblical theology, and at the same time a theological criterion for the spiritual or christian sense of the Old Testament. This would mean, not a valuing of any part of the Old Testament simply for itself (within christian theology); not necessarily a valuing of every part or theme of the Old Testament; but a valuing of precisely those themes which the apostolic Church itself saw as (in the geometrical sense) 'produced' by or extrapolated into Christ, as transformed and transcended by him, as fulfilled in Christ and his Church; the themes which the apostolic Church wove into the New Testament.

Indeed, the perspective can be widened (though this goes beyond a biblical theology), without questioning the unique and privileged place accorded to Israel by the Father of Our Lord Jesus Christ. If God's grace, which is the grace of Christ, presses upon and draws all men, and is what evokes their characteristically human experience, then one must see other human witness, especially overt religious witness, as a *praeparatio evangelica*, a preparation for the Gospel. The Fathers have a superb allegory: Adam (man) is shattered into pieces by the fall; Christ gathers the pieces of Adam that are scattered throughout human history, and moulds them once more into one.[12]

It has recently become fashionable in some circles to say that biblical theology is 'out', and radical theology is 'in'; that a constantly improving biblical theology is being addressed to a world (or Church) that has ceased to listen. Well, there is certainly place and need for 'radical' questions that are addressed to theology from out of the world's concerns and needs. But addressed to what? Radical questions or statements cannot form a theology of their own; they are often the opposite of what their chosen name implies, viz rootless; left to themselves they are superficial. Certainly, it was naïve to think (if anyone did) that the Bible has 'a' theology, one theology running through its witness of perhaps 1800 years. The New Testament itself has not got 'one theology', if by that is meant a single systematic conceptual pattern: it has many christologies, many soteriologies, it even has more than one mariology. It was an important stage forward to recognize more and more clearly the difference between hebraic and hellenic thought-patterns, and to come to grips with the various New Testament theologies; but any effort to construct on this process 'a' theology of the New Testament was doomed to failure. Nor, had it succeeded, is it immediately obvious that hebraic thought-patterns are necessarily better

for expressing the Gospel than hellenic ones, scripture (in
that sense) necessarily better than tradition. But it could be
that we have reached the point where a real biblical theology
is in fact on the way in. Without an agreed biblical theology,
there can neither be scripture in the light of tradition, nor
tradition in the light of scripture. There can be no criterion
of christian truth.

NOTES

1. H. de Lubac, sj, *Exégèse Mediévale*, 4 Vols, Paris, Aubier, 1959-1964.

2. It was at the same time recognised that parts of the Bible (Psalms,
Song of Songs) were themselves figurative, and a problem arose over whether
such incidents as the sun standing still at Jericho were literal or figurative.
As far as possible the Old Testament was taken as literally true. The method
demanded this.

3. *In Paslm* 79:1: 'Totum omnium scripturarum mysterium, Christum et
ecclesiam.' Again: 'For no other reason was all that we read in Holy Scripture written before the Lord's coming, than that his coming should be
heralded (*commendaretur*) and the future Church foreshadowed' (*De catech
rudibus*, 3.6).

4. 'Spiritus ipsius litterae, Christus': John Scotus Erigena, *In Ioann*, fr 2
(PL 122, 331).

5. The use of Fr Bernard Lonergan's terms is intentional!

6. *De Divina Revelatione*, 16, quoting Augustine, *Quaest in Hept*, 2.73:
Deus ita sapienter disposuit ut novum in vetere lateret et in novo vetus
pateret.

7. Haimo of Auxerre, *In Ap* II (PL 117, 1008): quod lucet in vetere testa-
mento hoc fulget in novo.

8. *In Matt*, 10:14

9. *Adv Haer*, 4.34.1: omnem novitatem attulit seipsum afferens.

10. H. de Lubac, op. cit, pp 324-328.

11. N. Lohfink, *The Christian Meaning of the Old Testament*, London
1969; P. Grelot, *Sens chrétien de l'Ancien Testament*, Paris, Aubier, 1962.

12. Augustine, *In Psalm*, 95, quoted by H. de Lubac, *Catholicism*, Burns
and Oates, 1950, pp 213-14.